# STUDIES
# IN SPENSER, MILTON,
# AND THE THEORY OF
# MONARCHY

# STUDIES
# IN SPENSER, MILTON,
# AND THE THEORY OF
# MONARCHY

**RUTH MOHL**

*Associate Professor of English, Brooklyn College*
*The City University of New York*

FREDERICK UNGAR PUBLISHING CO.
*NEW YORK*

*Printed in the United States of America*

Library of Congress Catalog Card No. 62-10898

*To the memory of*
PROFESSOR HARRY MORGAN AYRES

# PREFACE

THE PURPOSE of this book of studies is probably quite clear from the titles and contents of the individual essays. Though at first glance they may seem to have little in common, they are all concerned with problems of interpretation of medieval and Renaissance literature and are, therefore, in many ways unified. I have put them together because each one, I believe, sheds some light on the others. Those written last are, in fact, direct outgrowths of the earlier ones. All aim to re-study problems, some of them centuries old, which need re-interpretation on the basis of new evidence or on the basis of evidences newly associated. It is to be hoped that such re-interpretations may prove serviceable to students and teachers of Spenser, Milton, and their times as well as to critics and scholars, who know the values, in literary interpretation, of the historical approach.

I am glad of this opportunity to express my thanks to those who have helped to make these studies possible. They are the result, in part, of questions asked by students in my Spenser and Milton classes, many of whom have found the study of Spenser and Milton the exciting and timely adventure that it should be. I am grateful to them for providing a practical and immediate incentive for turning the desire to answer such questions into action. My great indebtedness to medieval and Renaissance scholars is evident throughout the book, and I shall not attempt, therefore, to name them here. I am grateful to the Syndics of the Cambridge University Press for permission to quote from B. E. C. Davis' *Edmund Spenser;* and to the Clarendon Press of Oxford University for their generous permission to quote from C. L. Wrenn's "On Re-reading Spenser's Shepheardes Calender" in *Essays and Studies by Members of the English Association,* Volume XXIX (1943), from Douglas Bush's *English Literature in the Earlier Seventeenth Century, 1600–1660,* and from R. Newton Flew's *The Idea of Perfection in Christian Theology.* I am also indebted to Chatto and Windus for permitting me to quote from Sir

Herbert Grierson's *Cross Currents in English Literature of the Seventeenth Century;* and to the Editor of *PMLA* for permission to reprint the article on "Theories of Monarchy in *Mum and the Sothsegger*" from Volume LIX (March, 1944). I am grateful to the staffs of the University of Minnesota Library, the James J. Hill Reference Library of St. Paul, the Columbia University Library, and the New York Public Library for their many helpful services.

My indebtedness, in largest measure, will always be to Professor Harry Morgan Ayres, whose sudden death on November 20, 1948, came as a shock and a great loss to all of us who had the privilege of knowing him as teacher and friend and of working under his guidance in medieval and Renaissance fields. His stimulating personality, his warm human interest in how we were "getting on," his breadth of learning, his keen critical sense and careful objectivity in research, his sensitivity to life in all its phases made him an inspiring guide indeed; and his remarkable gift of words made it possible for him to illumine whole centuries in a single apt phrase. To hear him read "out of the olde bokes" was to live in days long past. Fortunately for us, some of those readings have been recorded as a source of permanent profit and delight. Unfortunately his varied interests and activities prevented his recording in print as much of his profound insight and felicity of phrase as we should have liked to find thus preserved, but we remember them with gratitude and seek to pay a small part of the debt we owe in such inadequate but heartfelt dedications.

R. M.

*Brooklyn College*
June 27, 1949

# PREFACE TO THE SECOND PRINTING

IN THE TWELVE YEARS since these studies were first printed, many books and articles have appeared to aid in the understanding of the various aspects of the work of Spenser and Milton. Medieval studies have also provided further background for the interpretation of such a poem as *Mum and the Sothsegger*. It is impossible here to list all of those that have proved most valuable to me, but I should like to comment briefly on a few that have influenced my thinking concerning the studies here reprinted.

The crux of the problem concerning Spenser's Rosalinde and Diggon Davie seems to lie in the nature of the relationship between Spenser and the Sidneys. A. C. Judson, Spenser's American biographer, in his study of *Sidney's Appearance,* Indiana, 1958, reiterates his belief that "Spenser knew Sidney well" during Spenser's service as secretary to the Earl of Leicester. Some American scholars, however, question the existence of any friendship between them, apparently because of difference in rank. English scholars, on the other hand, seem to have no trouble in accepting the idea of such a friendship. A new life of Sidney, John Buxton's *Sir Philip Sidney and the English Renaissance,* London, 1954, is an example of the kind of acceptance an English biographer gives to the theory of a close relationship. This book, widely acclaimed for its "thorough and graceful scholarship," was the result, not of reading secondary sources, but of journeys to many libraries in several countries, where Sidney himself had been and to which he had written. The archives of Venice, Padua, Milan, Leyden, London, Oxford, Cambridge, and Penshurst yielded evidence. That Renaissance poets, including Spenser, looked to Sidney for the aid of his critical taste and judgment and enjoyed his hospitality at Penshurst as well as Mary Sidney's at Wilton, Buxton does not doubt. He implies also that, without knowing Sidney, Spenser could not have written so glowingly of the "secret ravishment" by which Sidney stole "all men's hearts." Sidney's friendship was by no means restricted to those of his own class, as the numerous friends and acquaintances he made abroad and in England prove. Buxton speaks of the envy with which later writers like Crashaw and Aubrey still looked back to the meetings of the poets at Penshurst or Wilton, with Spenser among them—much as Philip Sidney, in *The Sidneys of Penshurst,* London, 1901, speaks of the "extraordinary" roll of men and women who enjoyed such hospitality, "kings, queens, poets, princesses, soldiers, statesmen," and adds that "Here Spenser wrote a portion of his *Shepherd's Calendar."* Anyone who has visited beautiful Penshurst can have little trouble in believing that, among the guests at the tables in the long dining-hall, the Bishop of Rochester, the diocese in which Penshurst lies, and his gifted young secretary may have been found. The tone of Spenser's dedication of the *Shepheardes Calender* to Sidney implies, says Buxton, that "Spenser was by then well acquainted with Sidney." If some critics, like A. C. Hamilton in his excellent article on "The Argument of Spenser's *Shepheardes Calender"* in *ELH* for September, 1956, find the attempt to identify historical allusions in the eclogues a "perverse" and trivial pursuit, one can only remind them that Spenser himself challenges the reader to such inquiry and that one seldom reaches "universal" truths without first mastering the "particular." For the biographer and the historian, the "particular" truths are of prime importance. One may also note that Buxton remarks on how "These ingenious tricks with names commended themselves to Sidney's contemporaries in every country." In France, for example, puns were made on Sidney's name by calling him the "Cygne" or Swan. To Greville, Mary Sidney was Myra, and he described himself as Myraphill, her lover.

John Danby's study of Spenser in *Poets on Fortune's Hill,* London, 1952, similarly finds ample reason for a close association between Spenser and Sidney in Spenser's service as secretary to the Earl of Leicester and later to Lord Grey of Wilton. A sixteenth-century nation, he points out, needed public servants who had a classical education, a knowledge of languages and of history, and ability in performing state duties. Spenser, he asserts, was such a man. Not only his literary genius but also his general culture, his connection with "an house of auncient fame," and especially his capacity for conducting public affairs would give Spenser ready access into the Sidney-Leicester-Raleigh world. Danby, like Buxton, describes the Great House of Sidney's day as a "center of culture in its own right, independent of the Court," where a new literature was being created sufficient to give England a place in the Renaissance beside France and Italy.

The humanistic interpretation of *Paradise Lost,* which I have discussed in the two essays on Milton, is that of most critics, as is shown in a number of studies that have appeared in the last decade. Most significant, it seems to me, is Professor Tillyard's treatment of "The Crisis of *Paradise Lost"* in his *Studies in Milton,* London, 1951. "I begin with the assumption," he says, "that Adam, or Adam and Eve, are hero"; he concludes that it is the true heroism in their repentance and reconciliation with God that is the theme of *Paradise Lost,* and not their fall. In the very interesting comparison by Dick Taylor, Jr., in *Tulane Studies in English,* Volume X (1960), of Milton's treatment of the fall with the earlier harsh, even cruel, despairing treatments, the great change in the story as told by Milton is made very clear. The moral and spiritual victory of Adam and Eve, not their degradation, is stressed, with numerous quotations from *Paradise Lost.* Other similarly optimistic studies are those of William Madsen (1958), F. T. Prince (1958), John E. Parish (1959), and John M. Steadman (1959), all cited by Professor Taylor. Nor is this interpretation limited to English-speaking critics. In 1956 Richard Heinrich Grün's *Das Menschenbild John Miltons in Paradise Lost* appeared in Heidelberg, asserting that, without the human pair and the drama of their fall and regeneration, the epic would be "meaningless mythology." For a German scholar, as one can easily see, such an interpretation has profound meaning and promise.

This interpretation provides ample response, it seems to me, to the traditionalists, who regard the fall as the all-important theme of

*Paradise Lost* and therefore find Books XI and XII "poetically on a much lower level" than the rest of the epic. Kenneth Muir in *John Milton,* London, 1955, so analyzes Milton's conclusion, and J. B. Broadbent, in *Some Graver Subject. An Essay on Paradise Lost,* London, 1960, says that the "decay of the poetry" in the last books prevents our regarding them as the "crisis" of the epic, and that the poem ends in a lack of force. In the brief but penetrating study of *Milton, the Poet* by Professor A. S. P. Woodhouse, Toronto, 1955, the human aspects of the poem are minimized by the declaration that Adam, the protagonist of the epic, is defeated and that Christ is the hero. Since most of the action takes place on earth, and Christ is not, as yet, an earthly inhabitant, it is difficult to see how Christ can be called the hero. In the brief epic *Paradise Regained,* Christ is, of course, the hero, but his role in *Paradise Lost* is like that of the supernatural beings in Homer and Virgil, not that of the hero.

The theme of perfection has been discussed frequently in diverse forms since the day when William James wrote: "All our arts and sciences and institutions are but so many quests of perfection on the part of men." These studies record the never-ending concern for human excellence. It is no dead issue among theologians, political analysts, essayists—though assertions to the contrary do appear. Reinhold Niebuhr's attacks on perfectionism, according to some of his colleagues, may stem in part from the fact that "he has always been much tempted by it." It is the "divine imperatives" of perfectionism that save mankind from meaningless and useless judgments. Christianity is founded on faith in man's perfectibility. The history of perfection, when it is written, will show that only through the strength of his spiritual ideals has man endured. Milton's place in such a history is clear.

The poem *Mum and the Sothsegger,* though largely neglected, was analyzed in 1955 from a new point of view, that of a substantial "commentary on the problem of counsel." Arthur B. Ferguson, author of this analysis, in *Studies in the Renaissance,* Volume II, believes that the unknown author of *Mum* wrote to give advice to the king concerning the parliament, the council, the law courts, the clergy, and the people and to show the duty of all men of good will to speak out about the evils of the realm. The difference between medieval dependence on the simple remedy of counsel and the beginnings of modern political consciousness in Tudor England, "in terms of constructive policy, not merely the reporting of grievances," is clearly set forth. This new study is therefore a valuable contribution to our understanding of a difficult poem, which still has great significance, it seems to me, for the student of medieval theories about monarchy and the literature of estates.

This reprinting has made possible some essential revisions. Otherwise the text stands as it was, improved in appearance and readability.

R. M.

*Brooklyn College, City University of New York*
October 27, 1961

# CONTENTS

# THE GLOSSES CONCERNING
# SPENSER'S ROSALINDE

THE NUMEROUS efforts to determine the identity of Rosalinde[1] in Spenser's *Shepheardes Calender* have been directed mainly toward interpretation of the January, April, and June glosses, the Spenser-Harvey correspondence of April, 1580, and whatever facts are known about Spenser's life between 1570 and 1580. Some of the suggestions as to her identity[2] meet part of the requirements of those sources of information, but so far none has been shown to satisfy all of them. Nevertheless, one suggestion has been made that, it seems to me, does satisfy all the requirements. The reason why it has not been generally accepted is probably the fact that it has never been studied in relation to all the sources of information. The following review of the problem aims to show that Professor Percy W. Long's and Dr. J. J. Higginson's suggestion that Rosalinde may have been Mary Sidney[3] squares with all the known facts and especially with the parts of the January and April glosses that explain Spenser's choice of the name *Rosalinde* to hide the lady's identity.

In 1908, in his article suggesting that Rosalinde may have been Elizabeth North, Professor Long nevertheless included the following footnote: "It is remarkable that no one has suggested Sidney's sister, whose pastoral name *Clorinda* forms a passable solution of Rosa-

[1] As Professor Percy W. Long points out in his article on "Spenser's Rosalind," *Anglia*, XXXI (January, 1908), 95: "*Rosalinde* is the spelling to be used as a basis. It is the uniform spelling of the fifth quarto, which is Spenser's final edition. In all five quartos it is the spelling used by Harvey (Grosart, ed. Harvey, Huth Lib., I, 81–2)."

[2] They are reviewed in J. J. Higginson's *Spenser's Shepherd's Calendar in Relation to Contemporary Affairs* (New York: Columbia University Press, 1912), pp. 203–31; in H. S. V. Jones' *Spenser Handbook* (New York: F. S. Crofts, 1930), pp. 24–25; and in the Variorum Edition of Spenser's *Minor Poems* (Baltimore: Johns Hopkins Press, 1943), Appendix IV, pp. 651–55. They need not, therefore, be listed here.

[3] Long, "Spenser's Rosalind," *loc. cit.*, p. 82 n., and Higginson, *op. cit.*, pp. 230–31.

lind." [4] It was Professor Long, therefore, who first noted the plausibility of Mary Sidney's being Rosalinde. He did not try to fit her
name into the feigned name, however, as he did for Elizabeth North
and earlier for Elizabeth Carey.[5] In the text of his article he made the
following interesting comment on A. B. Grosart's hope of some day
finding a real Rose Dineley, to fit his resolution of the anagram:
"But why Rose? Call Rosalind by any other name, as Nora, Nellie,
Dora, Alice, or even Sally, and the anagram may be solved no less
readily, as Nora Disel, Nellie Dorsey, Alice Thorn. Yet after three
hundred years no real person has been adduced as Spenser's Rosalind!"

In 1912, after summarizing and rejecting earlier suggestions, Dr.
Higginson commented on two of the suggestions made by Professor Long as follows:

> At least, Elizabeth Carey or Mary Sidney must have been
> strangely like Rosalind as regards worldly position, intellectual
> attainments, and physical charm. Indeed Long has noticed that
> Rosalind is "a passable solution" for Clorinda, Mary Sidney's
> poetical name, by which she signed herself when she wrote the
> lament for her brother, and by which she was known to the poets
> of the time. But I will leave guessing to others. The conclusion
> of the whole matter must be that, although Rosalind was un-
> doubtedly a real person, her identity has up to the present time
> escaped discovery, a matter which can be counterbalanced by the
> knowledge that she probably resembled Lady Carey and the
> Countess of Pembroke in more ways than one, and that Spenser's
> attachment to her was that of an ambitious young poet to a lady-
> patron.[6]

Leaving the matter there, Dr. Higginson, like Professor Long, did
not attempt to apply the test of the glosses, though he did note [7]
Professor Long's inability to accept the view that Rosalinde is Lady

---

[4] "Spenser's Rosalind," *loc. cit.*, p. 82 n.

[5] Percy W. Long, "Spenser and Lady Carey," *Modern Language Review*, III (October, 1907), 257–67.

[6] Higginson, *op. cit.*, pp. 230–31.          [7] *Ibid.*, pp. 230–31 n.

Carey because "E. K. states that the name *Rosalinde* is an anagram," and there is "no way of making this answer the 'very name' of Elizabeth Carey." [8]

Today most students of Spenser would have little trouble in agreeing with the suggestion of Mary Sidney as Rosalinde so far as historical, biographical, and literary data are concerned. Her home in Kent; her station as a member of the Dudley and Sidney families; her reputation for charm and wit; [9] her marriage to the Earl of Pembroke on April 21, 1577, near the time when the *Shepheardes Calender* was being completed; as well as Spenser's expressions of admiration for and loyalty to her in the *Ruins of Time*,[10] in his sonnet to her prefixed to the *Faerie Queene,* in his reference to her as Clorinda, the "gentlest shepheardesse that lives this day," in *Astrophel*,[11] and in his praise in *Colin Clout* [12] of her "brave mynd," in whose "golden cofer all heavenly gifts and riches locked are"—are all familiar to the reader of Spenser and leave no doubt as to the eligibility of Mary Sidney for the role of Rosalinde.

Today there seems to be considerable agreement, too, as to a fairly close relationship between Spenser and the Sidneys [13] from the

[8] Long, "Spenser and Lady Carey," *loc. cit.*, p. 267 n.

[9] Cf. especially Malcolm W. Wallace, *The Life of Sir Philip Sidney* (Cambridge [Eng.]: University Press, 1915), pp. 156, 172, 188.

[10] The Dedication, the Envoy, and lines 316–22.

[11] Line 213.          [12] Lines 485–91.

[13] Cf. Wallace, *op. cit.,* pp. 105–10, 161, 228–29; E. de Selincourt, ed., *The Poetical Works of Edmund Spenser* (London: Oxford University Press, 1924), Intro., pp. xii–xiv; T. P. Harrison, Jr., "The Relations of Spenser and Sidney," *PMLA,* XLV (September, 1930), 712–31. Professor Harrison, after summarizing earlier views as to the Spenser-Sidney relationships and after comparing the work of the two poets, says: "The remarkable parallel in the chronology and nature of the two men's writings seems to point to a genuine intimacy." A German study by Mally Behler, "Die Beziehungen zwischen Spenser und Sidney," *Archiv für das Studium der neueren Sprachen und Literaturen,* CXLVI (1923), 53–59, does, as J. M. Purcell points out, *PMLA,* XLVI (September, 1931), 940, reach a somewhat different conclusion from that of Professor Harrison, mainly because of concern that Spenser be recognized as the greater poet. However, Behler does not deny them a "Bekanntschaft," speaks of their "lebhaftem literarischen Verkehr" in the years when the *Shepheardes Calender* was being written, and notes the similarity of their literary efforts and their great admiration for each other's work. In 1859 Thomas Keightley, in his article "On the Life of Edmund Spenser," *Fraser's Magazine,* LX (October, 1859), 410–22, went so far as to "suspect . . . that it was Sidney that proposed to him [Spenser] the subject of the *Calender,* which was evidently written in Kent, most probably at Penshurst." Professor A. C. Jud-

time of Philip Sidney's and Spenser's possible metting in Cambridge about 1571–72 [14] to their residence in Leicester House in 1579–80. By 1577 Mary Sidney was the Countess of Pembroke, maintaining her own London residence at Paul's Wharf, not far from Leicester House. Spenser's admiration for the house of Dudley is evident, of course, in the fact that he reviewed their history in the lost *Stemmata Dudleiana* and also in his *Ruins of Time*,[15] and his admiration for Sir Philip Sidney produced eulogies too numerous and too familiar to mention here. Politically, their Puritan sympathies formed a stronger bond than we are likely to realize today.

It remains, then, to show how the suggestion that Mary Sidney was Rosalinde meets the requirements of the January and April glosses on her name and on her identity as the "Widdowes daughter of the glenne." In the January gloss E. K. (probably Spenser himself and, if not, certainly authorized by Spenser) [16] says that "Rosalinde is also a feigned name, which being wel ordered, wil bewray the very name of hys love and mistresse." The phrase "very name" means "true name." The phrase "wel ordered" plainly means: "if the letters are put in their proper order." The gloss does not say,

son's *Life of Edmund Spenser* (Baltimore: Johns Hopkins Press, 1945), pp. 55–72, gives a full account of the evidence concerning the Spenser-Sidney-Leicester relationship and concludes (p. 59) that "however the connection was formed, there can be no doubt that Spenser for a time served Leicester and was on a friendly footing with Sidney, Dyer, and Rogers, frequented Leicester House, and had the entrée of the court."

[14] Wallace says that "contemporary evidence . . . leaves no reasonable doubt" of the fact that Sidney was a student at Cambridge as well as Oxford, probably in 1571–72, at a time when Spenser and Harvey were also at Cambridge, *op. cit.*, pp. 105–7.

[15] Cf. Josephine Waters Bennett, *The Evolution of the Faerie Queene* (Chicago: University of Chicago Press, 1942), chap. vii, on "Leicester's Place in Spenser's Plans."

[16] Cf. Agnes Duncan Kuersteiner, "E. K. Is Spenser," *PMLA*, L (March, 1935), 140–55, and D. T. Starnes, "Spenser and E. K.," *North Carolina Studies in Philology*, XL (April, 1944), 181–200, and Raymond Jenkins, "Who Is E. K.?" *Shakespeare Association Bulletin*, XX (January, 1945), 22–36, and XX (April, 1945), 82–94. As a result of this evidence, Paul E. McLane says that "it is practically certain that E. K. was Spenser," *PMLA*, LXII (December, 1947), 947. However, Robert W. Mitchner, "Spenser and E. K.: an Answer," *North Carolina Studies in Philology*, XLIII (April, 1945), 183–90, disagrees. C. L. Wrenn, "On Re-reading Spenser's Shepheardes Calender," *Essays and Studies by Members of the English Association*, XXIX (1943), 30–49, also believes that E. K. was not Spenser. He finds E. K. too "pompous and prosy," too much of "a stiff Protestant controversialist," to be Spenser.

however, that the name *Rosalinde* contains her whole "very name," nor does it say that it contains only her "very name." There is nothing in the gloss to prevent the poet's also having a secret or "counterfeict name" for the lady, and the rest of the gloss plainly hints, it seems to me, that he has such a secret name.[17] Just as Ovid called the lady Julia by the name *Corinna;* just as Aruntius Stella called his lady Violantilla by the names *Asteris* and *Ianthis;* just as Madonna Caelia of Italy hid her identity behind the name *Zima;* and as Petrona used the name *Bellochia,* Spenser suggests that he, too, has his own feigned name for his lady, a name that will be as much her true name as her family name because it mirrors her virtues as her own name does not. Further, in the April gloss, lest the reader forget the former statement, E. K. (or Spenser) recalls the name *Myrto,* which Theocritus gave his "dearling"; the name *Lauretta,* which Petrarch gave his "Goddesse"; and the name *Himera,* which the poet Stesichorus gave his "Idole." Thus the reader is led to search in the name *Rosalinde* for two names—a true name and a secret name.

If one looks in *Rosalinde* for the "very name" of Mary Sidney as well as a "counterfeict name," he will find them, though they must be "wel ordered" to be found. The letters *S-i-d-n-e* are easily detected; and there is no cause for concern in the omission of the letter *y,* for the earliest spelling of the family name was *Sidne,* not *Sidney.* In the last will and testament of Robert Earl of Leicester [18] the origin of the Sidney family in England is traced back to William de Sidne, who came from Anjou with Henry II and served Henry II as knight and chamberlain. The name in a Latin grant of the lands of Cesford and Lelleford to Roger, son of William de Sidne, is written *Roger Sidnei.* In sixteenth-century papers it appears as *Sidne, Sidnei, Sidneie,* and *Sidney.* Surely, therefore, no sixteenth-century

[17] Keightley, "On the Life of Edmund Spenser," *loc. cit.,* p. 413, makes the same observation. He concludes, however, quite contrary to the evidence, it seems to me, that "E. K. means no anagram" and that Rosalinde "was a purely ideal being like the aforesaid Corinna, like Beatrice, Laura, and others, like Drayton's Idea, Daniel's Delia."

[18] Arthur Collins, *Letters and Memorials of State . . . written and collected by Sir Henry Sidney . . . the famous Sir Philip Sidney, etc.* (London: printed for T. Osborne, 1746), II, 76 ff.

reader would miss the final *y* in Spenser's anagram. Now, after the five letters in *Sidne* are removed from *Rosalinde,* the letters *R-o-a-l* remain. When these letters are reordered, they, too, make a name, *Lora,* the French spelling for *Laura,*[19] whose fame as the subject of Petrarch's sonnets was being revived in the universities and at court in these particular years. Both Sidney and Spenser had probably written numerous sonnets by 1579, with Petrarch and the French sonneteers as their models. For Spenser, as for Petrarch, the graceful compliment implied in the laurel emblem would be fitting tribute to his lady. What could be more natural than that he should adopt that secret name, especially when it fitted so well into the pastoral name *Rosalinde,* in which *Sidne* was already so neatly concealed? With such double feigning, his secret would be even more secure. His expressed aim to insure that only "a few, but they be well sented, can trace him out" [20] would be achieved, even though, in the April gloss, he does help the reader to the extent of naming Petrarch's *Lauretta* along with the other secret names.[21]

In the April eclogue Hobbinoll's reference to Rosalinde as "the Widdowes daughter of the glenne" [22] and its accompanying gloss present another test of the plausibility of Mary Sidney's being Rosalinde, which, it seems to me, can be as reasonably resolved as that of the formation of her name. In fact, the gloss obviously lends

[19] Spenser's knowledge of French is pointed out by A. C. Judson, *The Life of Edmund Spenser* (Baltimore: Johns Hopkins Press, 1945), pp. 22–23, in his discussion of Spenser's translation from the French of the *Visions of Petrarch* and the *Visions of Bellay* from Van der Noot's *Theatre of Voluptuous Worldlings.*

[20] Epistle to Harvey, *Poetical Works of Edmund Spenser,* ed. J. C. Smith and E. de Selincourt, p. 418.

[21] An example of how persistent was the Petrarchan fashion of making puns on names and of listing ladies famous in history is Mercutio's taunting speech to Romeo, *Romeo and Juliet,* Act II, scene 4, ll. 38 ff., after Benvolio has announced his approach, "Here comes Romeo!" Mercutio replies: "Without his roe, like a dried herring. O flesh, flesh, how art thou fishified! Now is he for the numbers that Petrarch flowed in. Laura, to his lady, was but a kitchen-wench . . . Dido a dowdy; Cleopatra a gipsy; Helen and Hero hildings and harlots; Thisbe a grey eye or so, but not to the purpose. Signior Romeo, *bon jour!* There's a French salutation to your French slop." The shift to French at the end suggests the way by which much knowledge of Petrarch came to England and the reason why *Lora* would be as familiar as *Laura* to an Englishman.                                    [22] Ed. de Selincourt, p. 432, l. 26.

support to the theory that Rosalinde is Mary Sidney in its swift confession that

> the widowes daughter of the glenne . . . is rather sayde to coloure and concele the person then simply spoken. For it is well knowen, even in spighte of Colin and Hobbinoll, that shee is a Gentle woman of no meane house, nor endewed with anye vulgare and common gifts both of nature and manners: but suche indeede, as neede nether Colin be ashamed to have her made knowne by his verses, nor Hobbinol be greved, that so she should be commended to immortalitie for her rare and singular Vertues.[23]

Such praise of Rosalinde agrees entirely with Spenser's expression of his admiration for Mary Sidney and her "no meane house" elsewhere. The latter part of the gloss, then, presents no difficulty.[24] It is "the Widdowes daughter of the glenne" that needs explanation. The phrase sounds like a line from an old Scotch ballad; and indeed the *New English Dictionary* says that, so far as is known, the word *glenne* is used in the *Shepheardes Calender* for the first time in English literature, though it was common in Scotch and Irish literature earlier. Whether Spenser derived the phrase from some such rustic source or invented it himself, he plainly used it for pastoral effect. Why, however, should he call Mary Sidney's mother a "widow" and what did he wish to imply when he described her as living in a "glen"? The reader naturally looks for any known facts in the lives of the Sidney family, particularly that of Lady Sidney, which might have recommended such a description of her to the poet.

There are two reasons why anyone who knew the conditions of Lady Sidney's life in the 1560's and 1570's might have thought of her as widowed. Spenser, as secretary to John Young, Bishop of Rochester, the diocese of which Penshurst, home of the Sidneys,

---

[23] *Ibid.*, p. 433.

[24] Thomas Keightley's query, "On the Life of Edmund Spenser," *loc. cit.*, p. 413: "Why should Spenser be ashamed, or Harvey be jealous of her?" seems to me to be beside the point. What the gloss means is simply the opposite of what it says, namely, that they are both proud of her "rare and singular Vertues," much as Petrarch was proud of Laura's virtues.

was a part,[25] must have been aware of the problems and difficulties of so important a parishioner as Lady Sidney. In the first place, Sir Henry Sidney was so constantly in the service of the Court as to be seldom with his family, unless they visited him in Ireland or in Ludlow, where he served as Lord Deputy of Ireland and as Lord President of Wales.[26] Lady Sidney, apparently a woman of remarkable abilities,[27] was left in charge of the growing family in Penshurst and even of Sir Henry's affairs in London, so that later she had to maintain a residence there as well. As Professor Wallace says: "They must have been sad and lonely years for the young wife, beset with the bitter memories of recent events,[28] deprived of her husband's society, and living in a part of the country remote from her friends." [29] Then, in the second place, as if this loneliness were not enough, she had suffered a misfortune in 1560 that had made her isolation practically complete.[30] In October of that year English forces went to France to the aid of the French Protestants. They were under the command of the Earl of Warwick, whose military adviser on the expedition was Sir Henry Sidney, his brother-in-law. When Sir Henry returned a month later, to report to the Queen, he found that in his absence she had been dangerously ill of smallpox and that Lady Sidney had also contracted the disease while helping to nurse Elizabeth back to health. Elizabeth was left without a scar, but Lady Sidney must have been terribly marked, for Sir Henry, in a letter to Walsingham on March 1, 1583, wrote:

> When I went to Newhaven, I left her a full fair lady, in mine eye at least the fairest, and when I returned I found her as foul a lady as the small-pox could make her, which she did take by

[25] In John Thorpe's *Registrum Roffense* (London: W. and J. Richardson, 1769), a record of the affairs of the Bishopric of Rochester from earliest times, the church in Penshurst, in which most of the Sidneys are buried, is referred to as the "libera capella infra manerium de Penshurst" or as the "libera capella in parochia de Penshurste," pp. 136, 461, 462, 466, 469, 573.

[26] Cf. Wallace, *op. cit.*, pp. 10, 15, 16, 21–22, 74–75, 84–85, 150, 363.

[27] *Ibid.*, pp. 17, 20, 70–71, 363.

[28] Such as the disasters to the Dudleys after the Lady Jane Grey episode.

[29] Wallace, *op. cit.*, p. 15.    [30] *Ibid.*, pp. 21–22.

continual attendance of her Majesty's most precious person (sick of the same disease), the scars of which (to her resolute discomfort) ever since hath done and doth remain in her face, so as she liveth solitarily *sicut nicticorax* in *domicilio suo.*[31]

In other words, she was living "solitarily like a night-raven [a bird that cries at night] in her own home." After this experience, according to Professor Wallace, Lady Sidney went to Court only when commanded to do so by Elizabeth and spent most of her time in retirement at Penshurst with her children. To Lady Sidney the Queen showed no gratitude for her recovery, and the rest of her life Lady Sidney lived broken in health, harassed by debts, embittered, and alone. No more poignant figure emerges from the pages of the history of the Sidney family than that of this gifted, sensitive, high-born lady, whose service to the Crown brought her disfigurement and isolation and whose family, at the beck and call of Elizabeth, were often far from home. In a very real sense, therefore, she was a widow in her home in Penshurst; and it is even possible that she so described herself. Spenser's use of the term *widow* for Lady Sidney need not, therefore, seem familiar or disrespectful, but may have been rather an effort to ease the isolation by a bit of pastoral fiction. Being an intellectually gifted person, as Professor Malcolm Wallace's evidence shows her to have been, Lady Sidney would have been among the first to see the homely, but kindly humor in the phrase "the Widdowes daughter of the glenne."

Concerning Spenser's use of the word *glenne,* Professor Jefferson B. Fletcher, in 1907, made an observation that has considerable interest here because of its connection with Petrarch and his Laura. Professor Fletcher pointed out that the gloss on the word *glenne* misconstrues its meaning by calling it "a country Hamlet or borough," but that in Spenser's effort to "coloure and concele" his lady he had a "precise precedent" for the misconstruing in Petrarch's use of the term *borgo* to hint at the identity of his lady in Sonnet IV, "Quel

[31] Quoted by Wallace, *op. cit.,* p. 22.

ch' infinita providenzia et arte," of his *In Vita di Madonna Laura.*[32]
In that sonnet Petrarch compares the birth of Laura to that of the
Messiah.[33] Just as the Savior preferred Bethlehem to Rome as his
birthplace, so now, Petrarch says, God has chosen a little town as
the place in which to give a new light to the world in the form
of a fair woman. Petrarch's lines:

> Ed or di picciol borgo un Sol n' ha dato
> Tal, che Natura e'l luogo si ringrazia
> Onde si bella donna al mondo nacque

are translated as follows:[34]

> Now from a little town a sun he gave us
> Such that both nature and the place give thanks
> So fair a woman to the world was born.

"Whether by coincidence or not," says Professor Fletcher,

> E. K.'s "borough" exactly renders Petrarch's "borgo." In so far,
> the identification of Rosalind with a "hamlet or borough" agrees
> with Spenser's statement in "January" (ll. 49–52):

> > A thousand sithes I curse that carefull hower
> > Wherein I longd the neighbour towne to see,
> > And eke tenne thousand sithes I blesse the stoure
> > Wherein I sawe so fayre a sight as she . . .

> This sentiment itself, stereotyped by many imitators, harks back
> ultimately again to Petrarch's Sonnet XXXIX, *In Vita di Madonna
> Laura,* "Benedetto sia 'l giorno e'l mese e l'anno."

Such further evidence of Petrarchan influence on Spenser's pastoral
form makes the discovery of the name *Lora* in *Rosalinde* seem all
the more natural and acceptable. One wonders whether Spenser

[32] "The Widdowes Daughter of the Glenne," *Modern Language Notes,* XXII (February, 1907), 63.

[33] Cf. William Dudley Foulke, *Some Love Songs of Petrarch* (London: Oxford University Press, 1915), p. 213.

[34] *Ibid.* Foulke observes that "La Crusca defines a *borgo* as a street or collection of houses not surrounded by city walls, and more properly the suburbs or faubourg of a walled city."

meant to imply that the "neighbour towne" to which he went and where he saw and fell in love with Rosalinde was as sacred to him as the "piccolo borgo," the birthplace of Laura, was to Petrarch. In any event, whether *glenne* is to be interpreted as a "hamlet or borough" or whether it is thought of in its true meaning of "a secluded valley," as it is correctly used later in the *Faerie Queene*,[35] either interpretation is suitable as a description of the home of the Sidneys in the vales of Kent, and either would permit Mary Sidney to be Rosalinde.[36]

In connection with this explanation of the identity of Rosalinde, one's attention is naturally called to the paragraph in one of Harvey's letters to Spenser [37] in which he asks Spenser to imagine him [Harvey] "come into a goodly Kentishe Garden of your old Lords, or some other Noble man, and spying a florishing Bay [that is, Laurel] Tree there." Then Harvey bids Spenser recall Petrarch's address to the laurel. This recollection of Petrarch's words, says Harvey, may somewhat stir Spenser's imagination, "if any thing can be added to the loftinesse of his conceite, whom Mistress Rosalinde once reported to have all the Intelligences at commaundement, and an other time, Christened her Segnior Pegaso." With this preface Harvey introduces his own "Encomium Lauri," which, following the name of Rosalinde, suggests again the possibility of Spenser's having thought of Rosalinde as his "Laura," the "renowne of Prince and Princely Poeta alike." She is one whom Harvey himself "Faine wod . . . crave, might I so presume, some further acquaintance, O that I might? but I may not: woe to my destinie therefore." Instead, when the lady says, "Non omni dormio," he must say: "Yet Farewell, Farewell, the Reward of those, that I

---

[35] Book III, Canto vii, stanza 6.

[36] Concerning the word *glenne* Wrenn, "On Re-reading Spenser's Shepheardes Calender," *loc. cit.*, p. 47, says: "*Glenne* seems to have been introduced into English by Spenser in the *Shepheardes Calender* from the Scots, and 'E. K.' has evidently had to make a guess at its meaning, which he does clumsily with his 'a country Hamlet or borough.' " If Spenser, and therefore E. K., were working in a Petrarchan tradition, their gloss would not be a "clumsy" rendering of *glenne*, but a deliberate adaptation of Petrarch's setting for Laura in a "piccolo borgo" and at the same time a clever compliment and concealment of the identity of Spenser's Rosalinde.

[37] Ed. de Selincourt, p. 625.

honour." Again there is nothing in Harvey's lines that could not refer to sixteen-year-old Mary Sidney, for whom a suitor forty years old was fit husband because he had the station and wealth that Spenser and Harvey lacked.

From another passage in the Spenser-Harvey correspondence, Mr. Douglas Hamer finds in the line "Per tuam Venerem altera Rosalindula est" the meaning that Spenser had in March, 1580, married another Rosalinde, having lost the first one.[38] Dr. Theodore Banks, translating the line differently, concluded that "altera Rosalindula" referred, not to "another Rosalinde," but to "a changed Rosalinde," and that hence Spenser married the original Rosalinde.[39] Such a conclusion is, of course, untenable if Mary Sidney is Rosalinde, and the "altera Rosalindula" must remain "another Rosalinde," as Mr. Hamer translated it.

In *Colin Clouts Come Home Againe,* lines 907–51, Spenser's account, fifteen years later, of "faire Rosalind" as the shepherdess "of divine regard and heavenly hew," whom he loved without success because he "lookt so hie" and whom he loved so well "that hers I die," suggests that lines 464–79, expressing his vassallage to "one, whom all my dayes I serve," must also refer to Rosalinde. He could scarcely declare his undying love for more than one lady in the same poem. If lines 464–79 do refer to Rosalinde, and if Rosalinde is identified as Mary Sidney, then a question naturally arises concerning the speech of Melissa directly following, in which she says, "Who *else* [at Court] vouchsafed thee of grace?" and Colin's reply:

> They all (quoth he) me graced goodly well,
> That all I praise, but in the highest place,
> Urania, sister unto Astrofell.

The question and the answer would seem to imply that Rosalinde and Mary Sidney are two different persons, instead of one. On the other hand, knowing Spenser's earlier care in concealing the identity

---

[38] "Spenser's Marriage," *Review of English Studies,* VII (July, 1931), 271–90.
[39] "Spenser's Rosalinde: a Conjecture," *PMLA,* LIII (June, 1937), 335–37.

of Rosalinde, for literary effect no less than for personal reasons, we can understand why he saw no reason to reveal it here for all the world to see. Instead, it seems significant to me that his profession of everlasting devotion to Rosalinde immediately precedes his outstanding praise of Mary Sidney, as if the two were so closely associated in his mind that he could not separate them. And merely tucking in the little word *else* would serve again to "coloure and concele" Rosalinde's identity, as Petrarch had zealously concealed that of his Laura. After all, as the Countess of Pembroke Mary Sidney could no longer be exactly the same Rosalinde whom he had fallen in love with in the "neighbour towne" some twenty years before. As one of the "nymphs" in the "retinewe" of Elizabeth, she might, with the rest, do him honor; but she was no longer the "gentle mayd" to whom he first pledged allegiance. Nevertheless, she had remained his ideal and was always to remain so. In their long devotion to an ideal, the parallel between Spenser and Petrarch is again striking, for, like Spenser, Petrarch loved Laura for more than twenty years, until her death, and his Laura was probably, like Rosalinde, a married woman, for he refers to Laura as *donna* or *madonna* or *mulier,* never as *puella* or *donzella,* and, according to William Dudley Foulke, her "resistance to the passion of her lover during twenty years of devotion, retaining his affection yet denying her favours, is much more easily explained by the insurmountable obstacle of her marriage than in any other way." [40] Of course, by the time Spenser wrote *Colin Clouts Come Home Againe* he, too, was soon to woo and wed again, so that his own marriages, as well as Rosalinde's, made her only an ideal. Later the Countess of Pembroke translated Petrarch's *Triumph of Death,* thus showing that she shared the admiration of her time for the creator of Laura.

The conclusion that such was the way in which Spenser hit upon the name *Rosalinde* to mystify his readers and that Mary Sidney was the object of his pastoral affection seems to be the simplest hypothesis by which to explain all the phenomena and hence seems

[40] Foulke, *op. cit.,* p. 205.

inescapable. The fact that some sense can be made of the glosses
by so simple a reordering of the letters of her name adds further
weight to the biographical and literary evidence available and provides a solution more satisfactory than any of the other suggestions
made so far. Such suggestions as those recommending Rose Dineley,
Rosa Linde, Eliza Horden, Eliza North, Samuel Daniel's sister,
even though they approximate the requirements of the anagram,
have little meaning since the identity of the ladies is difficult or
impossible to establish. E. K. says that Colin Clout is "the Authour
selfe," that Hobbinoll is "Mayster Gabriel Harvey," and that "by
the names of other shepheardes, he covereth the persons of divers
other his familiar freendes and best acquayntaunce." [41] To have
gone far afield to find his shepherdess and to have chosen someone
unknown to the rest would have left the sixteenth-century reader
as well as the modern reader apathetic, to say the least. To choose
someone in "the inner circle," whom he may have loved—or may
not have loved, but whom he much admired and wished to honor
—was to stir the imagination "till the worlds dissolution." [42] No
one seems to fit such requirements so well as Mary Sidney.

[41] September gloss, ed. de Selincourt, p. 455.
[42] December gloss, ed. de Selincourt, p. 467.

# SPENSER'S DIGGON DAVIE

IN THE LIGHT of some of the most recent studies of Puritanism,[1] in all its phases, and as a result of our better understanding of the international and clerical nature of sixteenth-century Puritanism as distinguished from the national and sectarian nature of seventeenth-century Puritanism,[2] such evidences of the movement in the sixteenth century as the four "moral-satyrical" eclogues of Spenser's *Shepheardes Calender* take on new meaning and significance. Of all the shepherds who there discuss the state of the Church in the last half of the sixteenth century, none is better informed or more outspoken in his indictment of its faults than Diggon Davie in the September eclogue, the last of the four eclogues devoted to the Church. The identity of Diggon Davie, therefore, becomes a matter of considerable interest to the reader. In the September eclogue he is questioned by Hobbinoll, who, according to one of E. K.'s September glosses, is "Mayster Gabriel Harvey." *Hobbinoll,* says E. K. (perhaps Spenser himself)[3] in his January gloss, is a "fained country name, whereby, it being so commune and usuall, seemeth to be hidden the person of some of his very speciall and most familiar freend." Lest the reader forget the fact that these familiar names are used to represent familiar friends, E. K. adds, in another September gloss, "As also by the name of other Shepheardes, he covereth the persons of divers other his familiar freendes and best

---

[1] Notably M. M. Knappen's *Tudor Puritanism* (Chicago: University of Chicago Press, 1939); William Haller's *The Rise of Puritanism* (New York: Columbia University Press, 1938); A. S. P. Woodhouse, *Puritanism and Liberty* (London: J. M. Dent, 1938); Ralph Barton Perry, *Puritanism and Democracy* (New York: Vanguard Press, 1944); Perry Miller, *The Puritans* (New York: American Book Company, 1938); H. W. Schneider, *The Puritan Mind* (New York: Henry Holt and Company, 1930); Arthur Barker, *Milton and the Puritan Dilemma* (Toronto: Toronto University Press, 1942); Christina H. Garrett, *The Marian Exiles* (Cambridge [Eng.]: University Press, 1938).

[2] Cf. Knappen, *op. cit.,* Preface, p. v.          [3] See above, p. 4, n. 16.

acquayntaunce." As a result of Diggon Davie's fervent denunciation of Church practices and as a result of his association with
Harvey under a "fained country name," so "commune and usuall"
that it, too, must be taken to represent one of Spenser's and Harvey's
"familiar freendes and best acquayntaunces," the reader naturally
wonders as to the identity of Diggon Davie; and it is the purpose
of this paper to show that of all Spenser's and Harvey's acquaintances
none fits the role so well as Philip Sidney. A few other candidates
have been suggested, none of whom, it seems to me, has all the
necessary requirements. I shall first try to show why they seem
unlikely and then present the evidence for Sidney's being Diggon.

So far as I have been able to discover, there have been only four
persons suggested for the role in the three hundred and fifty years
since the *Shepheardes Calender* was published. In 1882, in his edition of Spenser's *Complete Works,* A. B. Grosart proposed John
Van der Noot as follows: "The very palpable provincialism of the
speaker must be set down as intended to represent Van der Noot's
broken or imperfect or book-learned English." [4] Since Van der
Noot was a Flemish refugee, whose Calvinist activities in Antwerp
forced him to flee from the Spanish authorities to England in 1567
and who wrote as part of his *Theater of Voluptuous Worldlings*
a bitter attack against Rome, he fits the role of Diggon Davie so
far as religious and political sympathies are concerned; and no
doubt, as Grosart asserts, the errors in Diggon's speech are used
to suggest a character ignorant of correct English. However, the
errors need not represent those of a foreigner, and Spenser plainly
indicates that Diggon is an Englishman who has been "in forraine
countryes," who has returned home and who now recounts what
he has seen to his old friend Hobbinoll. Plainly Van der Noot will
not do.

Frederick G. Fleay in his *Guide to Chaucer and Spenser* thought
it probable that Diggon Davie was Thomas Churchyard, the poet,[5]
apparently because Churchyard wrote a poem called *Davy Dickar's*

---

[4] Volume I, p. 26.

[5] Cf. J. J. Higginson, *Spenser's Shepherd's Calender in Relation to Contemporary
Affairs* (New York: Columbia University Press, 1912), p. 188.

*Dream.* However, since there is no evidence that Churchyard, soldier of fortune, had the opportunity or the desire to study political and religious conditions abroad, and since he was not known as a "familiar freende" of Spenser, he, too, is a most unlikely candidate. Churchyard's having used the name *Davy Dickar* need have no connection with Spenser's Diggon Davie, since the name was a common appellation for a laborer from the time of *Piers Plow-man* on.[6]

In 1912, in his study of *Spenser's Shepherd's Calendar in Relation to Contemporary Affairs,* Dr. J. J. Higginson, having rejected Van der Noot and Churchyard because they were not clergymen—though why they must be clergymen I do not know, since shepherds in pastoral literature are often poets rather than clergymen, and surely Hobbinoll and Colin Clout were not clergymen—chose a candidate from the ranks of the clergy: Richard Greenham, vicar of Dry Drayton.[7] *Diggon,* Dr. Higginson pointed out, is a corruption of *Richard;* and *Davie,* he thought, might be a corruption of *Drayton* —an observation less easy to follow. The "farre countrye" to which this Diggon Davie had traveled would have to be London, since Richard Greenham never traveled farther. For several reasons, how-ever, he is not an acceptable candidate. In the first place, no biographer of Spenser has found evidence to prove that Greenham was a friend or acquaintance of Spenser. Moreover, the character and experience of Greenham scarcely fit those of Diggon Davie.[8] After leaving Cambridge, to become rector of Dry Drayton, he served that poor parish for two decades and moved to London long after the *Shep-*

---

[6] The name *Degon* occurs in the fourteenth-century *Mum and the Sothsegger,* E. E. T. S., orig. ser., 199 (London: Oxford University Press, 1936), p. 22, l. 351; and the names *Degon* and *Dobyn* occur in the same text, p. 23, l. 362. In his edition of *Piers Plowman,* W. W. Skeat printed a part of the poem under the title *Richard the Redeles* with the following note on *Degon* and *Dobyn* ([Oxford, 1886], II, 302): "Evidently Diggon and Dobbin, both common names for country bumpkins, here used in contempt of the upstarts who used to burst in men's doors and rob them." In *Piers Plowman, Dauwe* is used frequently for *Davie* or *David.* George Gascoigne, mentioned in a November gloss of the *Shepheardes Calender* as a "wittie gentleman, and the very chefe of our late rymers," in 1576 wrote his *Steele Glas,* in which he looks forward to the time "When Davie Dicker diggs and dallies not," (l. 1,078). No doubt Gascoigne's poem was as familiar to Spenser as Churchyard's, or more so.

[7] Higginson, *op. cit.,* p. 188.          [8] Cf. Knappen, *op. cit.,* pp. 382–86.

*heardes Calender* was written. He did not travel abroad, as Diggon did. Nor was he the ardent controversialist that Diggon Davie is. Though a Puritan, he was famed for his objections to controversy, urging the controversialists in the Protestant schism to love one another. To his Bishop he described himself as "a sole poor country-man, a young scholar," [9] not competent to dispute with his older superiors. He had learned by experience, he said, "that dissension of reasons doth cause alienation of affections." [10] He gained a wide reputation as a peacemaker, "arbitrating the quarrels of the conten-tious countryside." [11] He was also famed for his charity, giving away most of his living. Diggon Davie, on the other hand, went abroad because: "In forrein costes, men sayd, was plentye . . . I dempt there much to have eeked my store." [12]

The latest candidate for the role of Diggon Davie is that of Viola Blackburn Hulbert, who, in July, 1942,[13] suggested that he may have been Richard Davies, Bishop of St. David's in Wales from 1561 to 1582. Mrs. Hulbert had three main reasons for her conclu-sions. First, she found in the use of *her* for *you, I,* and *he* in the opening speeches and in the use of *g* in *Diggon* instead of the *c* in *Diccon* two peculiarities of Welsh dialect in Tudor times. Secondly, she believed that Wales fulfills the requirements of the term *forraine countryes* of the gloss—though how Wales can be considered more than one country is not clear. Thirdly, she found in the character and career of Bishop Davies the requirements for the role of Diggon Davie. He was an ardent Protestant; he was poor; his career was "not beyond reproach," and after his death he was accused by his successor "of simony and of impoverishing the diocese to his own financial gain." Also, the evils in the Church mentioned by Diggon Davie could all be found in Wales, since Bishop Davies criticized them in his diocesan reports, and "if one compares them with the content of other diocesan reports they can be taken as fairly repre-sentative of the country."

[9] Quoted in *ibid.,* p. 383.     [10] *Ibid.*
[11] *Ibid.,* p. 384.     [12] September eclogue, lines 28 and 30.
[13] "Diggon Davie," *Journal of English and Germanic Philology,* XLII (July, 1942), 349–67.

In these suggestions there are, I believe, a number of difficulties, and the first is that of the dialect. Why, if Diggon reports on his journey in Welsh dialect,[14] does Hobbinoll, who has not been to Wales, have the same dialectic peculiarity? In fact Hobbinoll, not Diggon, begins the use of *her*. Moreover, the *g* in *Diggon* is western English as well as Welsh, as is clear from its use in the west country dialect of *Mum and the Sothsegger*.[15] C. L. Wrenn, in his analysis of Spenser's language in 1943,[16] says,

> I never tire of reading aloud this dialogue between Hobbinol and Diggon Davie, who for the nonce appear here as real country folk *from the south-west of England*,[17] whose racy spoken dialect (though of course Spenser does not keep it up) is marked not by its vocabulary as rustic, but by its very texture, its accidence and syntax. . . . This, read aloud in a resonant *south-western accent,* seems to me delightfully effective.

Later he again refers to the rusticity as that of the southwest: "I have already referred to what is perhaps Spenser's best rustic effort, the opening dialogue of the September eclogue. Here the use of *her* as a nominative and the general effect *are clearly from south-western speech.*"[18]

Another difficulty with Dr. Hulbert's theory is, as I have said, the phrase *forraine countryes,* which plainly implies more than one country. And why should Bishop Davies report concerning condi-

[14] Dr. Hulbert states, on the authority of Professor T. Gwynn Jones, "Tudor Welshmen's English," *Y Cymmrodor,* XXIX (1919), 56–69, that the stage Welshman in the Tudor period used *her* for "almost any pronoun." Professor Jones does not actually generalize to that extent, since (p. 59) he says: "Constructions of this kind and others are much more numerous in Decker's play (*Patient Grisill*)" than in the other three plays on which his study is based, namely, Shakespeare's *Henry V* and *Merry Wives of Windsor* and Jonson's Mask *For the Honour of Wales.* I find no evidence of such a use of *her* in Shakespeare's two plays and only one instance of it in Jonson's Mask. Sir Hugh Evans and Fluellen mispronounce words, misuse words, and make grammatical errors, but they do not confuse their pronouns. In Jonson's Mask some Welsh women use *her* for *it* on one occasion. From Dekker's play Professor Jones (p. 61) cites only eight cases of the use of *her,* and two of them are for *her* and *she.*

[15] See above, p. 17, n. 6.

[16] "On Re-reading Spenser's Shepheardes Calender," *Essays and Studies by Members of the English Association,* XXIX (1943), 43. Oxford: Clarendon Press, 1944.

[17] Italics are mine.  [18] Page 46.

tions in Wales to Gabriel Harvey? Was he, as E. K. insists that
Diggon Davie must be, one of Spenser's "familiar freendes and
best acquayntaunces"? The sense of rustic camaraderie between
Hobbinoll and Diggon is evident throughout the eclogue, even to
Hobbinoll's scolding Diggon for speaking so plainly. Would Harvey
have felt free to scold Bishop Davies, as he would have felt free
to speak to his friend Sidney, younger than Harvey by several
years? Moreover, if Bishop Davies was himself guilty of impoverishing his flock, how could he, as Diggon Davie, denounce others for
the same offense? Finally, if, as Dr. Hulbert says, the Catholics
in Wales were fewer in number than they were reported to be, and
if, as William Pierce states in his book on *John Penry,*[19] Catholicism
in Wales "passed peacefully away in its sleep," one may also ask
why Spenser should have bothered to satirize conditions in Wales
at all, when there was much richer material elsewhere.

The whole eclogue, it seems to me, is meant to be, as it plainly
indicates, a report on *world* conditions, both ecclesiastical and political, at a time when the two could scarcely be thought of separately
and when ambassadors to foreign countries, both lay and clerical,
often represented matters of both church and state without distinction between them. As Spenser says, "The shepheards swayne
you cannot wel ken, But it be by his pryde, from other men"; or
again, "Some say faith has declined because shepherds 'holden shame
of theyr cote.' " Such conditions, as well as the other abuses reported
by Diggon Davie, were Continental as well as English, and were
certainly not shown to advantage by stress on one rather remote
and comparatively insignificant Welsh diocese. The world, rather
than one country, is stressed throughout the eclogue, from the
reference in the Argument to Diggon's having gone into "a farre
countrye," through Hobbinoll's mention of Diggon's having "meas-
ured much grownd" and "wandred . . . about the world rounde,"[20]
through Diggon's reference to "tho countryes, whereas I have
bene,"[21] through his assertion that false shepherds stir up disputes

[19] London: Hodder and Stoughton, 1923.        [20] Lines 21–22.
[21] Line 32.

whereby "they sette all the world on fire," [22] through his determination to speak of "shepheards most what" [23] (that is, in general), through his lament that "the world is much war [that is, worse] then it wont," [24] to E. K.'s gloss that England has no wolves unless they be "brought from other countryes." The "forraine countryes" of the first gloss evidently refers to the rest of this "world," not to Wales alone, which could scarcely be thought of, either, as "forraine."

In April, 1947, Paul E. McLane [25] reviewed Dr. Hulbert's theory and sought to reinforce it by the addition of further evidence. He noted that Richard Davies was one of the Marian exiles in Frankfort from 1553 to 1557,[26] where some of the intimate and life-long friends of Bishop Young were also exiled; that after Davies' appointment as Bishop of St. Asaph, Wales, in 1560, he remained there, though returning to London on church duties in 1560, 1563, 1571, 1576; that one Mr. Edward Carey, a groom of her majesty's privy chamber, was notorious for his "long and merciless plundering" of the revenues of Davies' bishopric, though most of the faults charged to Davies (neglect of diocese, sale of livings, lavishness, and improvidence) were not revealed until after Davies' death, by some of his "disreputable and untrustworthy successors." Reasoning from these facts and from Dr. Hulbert's evidence, Dr. McLane sought to show that Spenser might have known Davies through Bishop Young; that the dialect in the eclogue would "immediately proclaim Diggon Welsh"; that in calling Davies Diggon Davie, Spenser "would be following his normal procedure in using outstanding prelates of the period in the ecclesiastical eclogues"; that the similarity of names would make the identification the "normal assumption"; that Diggon's laments of poverty as well as his emblem "would give point to Carey's robbery of Davies"; that Diggon's (that is, Davies') ambition to be enriched was "in a sense normal and legitimate to one of his calling," but that Spenser, while ad-

---

[22] Line 87.     [23] Line 104.     [24] Line 108.

[25] "Diggon Davie Again," *Journal of English and Germanic Philology*, XLVI (April, 1947), 144–49.

[26] Cf. Garrett, *op. cit.*, p. 141.

miring Davies for his opposition to the crown and for his attainments in poetry and biblical scholarship, may be satirizing him for having "set his heart on worldly possessions, since no ideal shepherd could have such a desire." Here the reasoning becomes difficult to follow, and one is prone to comment that it is easier to believe that Spenser admired Sidney because we know that he did. Dr. McLane admits that he has discovered no direct evidence of any relationship between Davies and Spenser. Nevertheless, he feels sure that Spenser's "extreme literalness in other portions of the *Calender*" would make it difficult for most of those in high political and ecclesiastical circles in 1579 to refrain from "leaping to the identification of Davies with Diggon Davie."

On the basis of Dr. McLane's own argument concerning Spenser's "extreme literalness" in reflecting contemporary affairs, one may fairly ask why we should ignore the numerous statements that it is "the world" about which he is writing, foreign countries as well as England. Nowhere is Wales even mentioned; and, as I have shown, the dialect is rustic English as well as Welsh. Though Davies was in Frankfort in 1553–57, his restricted exile there could scarcely be called wandering "about the world rounde"; and surely any news he could give of Frankfort in 1558 would be pretty old news by 1578. Moreover, Davies went to Wales in 1560 and stayed there except for occasional duties in London, whereas Diggon Davie says he is sorry he ever left England,[27] and intends now to look after his duties at home, "driven by neede to come home agayne." The argument that the names Diggon Davie and Richard Davies sound alike is not significant since the names Hobbinoll and Gabriel Harvey or Colin Clout and Edmund Spenser do not sound alike. It is true that when Spenser is representing shepherds who are prelates he does give them names that are derived from the real names, such as Algrind for Grindal and Morrell for Aylmer. But, as I have said before, the pastoral tradition began with poets as shepherds, and the introduction of clerical shepherds was a much later addition. Why may not Spenser have poet-shepherds as well

[27] Lines 56–67.

as ecclesiastics? Surely with Colin Clout and Hobbinoll he does. And why should he not have poet-shepherds conversing in the September eclogue after putting ecclesiastical shepherds together in the July eclogue? Such uniformity would be more natural than the mixing of poet-shepherds and ecclesiastical shepherds. The tone of the dialogue in the September eclogue would suit the decorum of poet-shepherds' talk; it is hard to think of it as the talk of poet and bishop. In line 124, moreover, Diggon is not talking of *himself* as being impoverished by the "bigge Bulles of Basan," but is simply reporting what the people are saying about the thefts from the clergy by rapacious rulers and courtiers everywhere. Nothing, so far, has been said to imply that England alone is meant. To be sure, all flagrant examples of despoliation in England as well as Wales would be suggested by Diggon's report, but why limit the meaning of his report to one country? As for Mr. Edward Carey's pilferings in Wales being the work of a "bigge Bull of Basan," it is difficult to think of so limited a scope for Spenser's satire. Dr. McLane's rather halfhearted defense of Bishop Davies' desire to be enriched raises the objection that Diggon's chief complaint is against the clergy who set their hearts on riches. Could a bishop have such ambitions and then complain of them in others? Altogether the identification of Diggon Davie as Bishop Davies seems to me untenable.

Keeping in mind all the requirements for the role of Diggon Davie, one next asks himself, Who, then, may he have been? There are several reasons, as I shall indicate, why Spenser probably had Philip Sidney in mind when he wrote the speeches of Diggon Davie. In the first place, Sidney fits very well the requirement of the gloss on Diggon Davie that he be a "very freend to the Author hereof." Today, as I have indicated in discussing the probability of Mary Sidney's being Rosalinde,[28] there is considerable agreement as to the fairly close relationship between Sidney and Spenser from 1571–72 to 1580. Moreover, the dedication of the *Shepheardes Calender* to Sidney makes it seem fitting that he should appear as a shepherd. It would seem strange, in fact, if he were not included.

[28] Cf. above, p. 3, n. 13.

The setting of the eclogues in Kent, home of the Sidneys, with which they were constantly identified, undoubtedly makes Sidney a better candidate than Van der Noot, Churchyard, Greenham, or Davies, none of whom was associated with Kent. Sidney's friendship for Harvey, about whom in a letter to Harvey dated October 5, 1579, Spenser says Sidney has asked for news "and so promised to doe againe," makes Sidney's conversation with Harvey in the September eclogue seem very natural indeed. Furthermore, the gloss stating that Diggon "had bene long in forraine countryes, and there seene many disorders" fits Sidney exactly. It suggests Sidney's three-year sojourn abroad, from 1572 to 1575, as well as his later journey in 1577, and qualifies him as Hobbinoll's informer. Sidney's one absorbing interest after his sojourn abroad was the cause of Continental Protestantism, the decline of which Diggon Davie discusses in the September eclogue. There was probably no one in England who knew so much about conditions abroad as he did.[29] Sidney was also like Diggon Davie in the fact that he hoped to find opportunity abroad for bettering his fortunes, probably as ambassador of the court of Elizabeth. Spenser himself was at one time about to go on such an embassy, for the Earl of Leicester, but for some reason did not go.[30] Though Diggon Davie "was bewitcht with vayne desyre, and hope to be enricht," he found that "it is nothing sich," just as Sidney did. Diggon Davie's emblem, *Inopem me copia fecit,* fits Sidney in more ways than one, for financially he was always hard-pressed, though so near the Queen, and politically, with a wealth of talents for service, he was never permitted suitable opportunity to use them.[31] The name *Diggon Davie,* with its connota-

[29] Cf. Malcolm W. Wallace, *The Life of Sir Philip Sidney* (Cambridge, [Eng.]: University Press, 1915), p. 183. See also A. Philip McMahon, "Sidney's Letter to the Camerarii," *PMLA,* LXII (March, 1947), 83–95.

[30] A. C. Judson, *The Life of Edmund Spenser* (Baltimore: Johns Hopkins Press, 1945), p. 60.

[31] Wallace, *op. cit., passim.* F. Kluge, O. Reissert, and C. H. Herford all point out (see Introductory Notes to the September Eclogue in the Variorum Edition of the *Minor Poems,* pp. 350–52) that "The general motive [in Spenser's poem] is that of Virgil's first Eclogue as developed in Mantuan's ninth." The shepherd's reason for traveling, i.e., his desire to better himself, and his disappointment in his quest are the same in all three. However, whereas Virgil and Mantuan have the stay-at-home and

tion of rustic laborer as digger or delver, from the days of *Piers Plowman* on, would surely please the fancy of Spenser and his friends if applied to Sidney; and the exaggerated rustic speech in the eclogue (not simply the use of *her* in the opening lines) would be most amusing in the mouth of one so cultured as Sidney. It has been pointed out [32] that Sidney said little about the *Shepheardes Calender* in his *Defence of Poesie,* as if that were an indication of Sidney's disregard for the significance of the work. He may have spoken of it only briefly because he himself was so much concerned with it—in dedication, in family references, and in the role of Diggon Davie. And undoubtedly Diggon Davie's frank criticism of Church and clergy would make his reserve even more likely. Finally, the fact that the following eclogue, the October eclogue, deals with the theme of poetry and mentions Spenser's *English Poet* in its Argument suggests an association in Spenser's mind between Sidney and poetry and himself.

Sidney's first experience with the sixteenth-century warfare between Catholics and Protestants on the Continent was St. Bartholomew's Massacre, which began on Sunday, August 24, 1572, and lasted for nearly a week. Sidney, as one of the retinue of the Earl of Lincoln, had arrived in Paris almost three months before the massacre occurred. From that time on, he was acutely sensitive to the religious troubles of Italy, Spain, France, Germany, and the Low Countries. As Professor Wallace says,

> He had gained a grasp of the complicated European political situation, not only as far as France, Spain, and the Netherlands were concerned, but in the German States, in Poland, Bohemia, and the Empire. He had gained this knowledge not only from books, though his historical reading had been very wide, but

---

prosperous shepherd tell of conditions in Rome to the wandering shepherd, Spenser gives the role of satirist to the wandering shepherd and amplifies the satire and adapts it to conditions in the Anglican Church. Sidney was advised by his friend Hubert Languet to stay away from the corrupting influences of Italy, especially Rome. Languet was distressed when Sidney visited Venice, Florence, and Genoa. Cf. Wallace, *op. cit.,* pp. 128, 137.

[32] Cf. E. A. Greenlaw, "The Shepheards Calender," *PMLA,* XXVI (September, 1911), 419–51.

by meeting personally and discussing affairs with the nobility, the statesmen, and the most famous literary men of Europe." [33]

In Germany he proposed a Protestant League and a Church Conference, much as the Lutheran princes of the early sixteenth century had proposed such a league to Henry VIII; and in a speech before the Emperor he advocated a general league against Rome and Spain. He visited William of Orange, who proposed that Sidney become Lord of Holland and Zealand through marriage with William's sister—a proposal that came to nothing, probably because Queen Elizabeth objected.[34] Sidney was now "personally acquainted with all the more prominent Protestant leaders on the Continent . . . and we hear much of his voluminous correspondence with them." [35]

With such a wealth of information and in the guise of Diggon, Sidney could speak plainly, as he dared not do in his own name during most of his life. Diggon's description of the shepherds (that is, clergy) who "robben one another and layen baytes to beguile her [that is, their] brother"; who either "bene ydle and still and leddè of theyr sheepe" or "bene false, and full of covetise and casten to compasse many wrong emprise," such as buying sheep from another's fold or cutting the shepherd's throat if he resists; whose underlings are as swelled with pride as a fat bull or a crowing cock; who "kindle coales of conteck and yre, wherewith they sette all the world on fire"; [36] who never themselves set a foot on the highway

---

[33] Wallace, *op. cit.*, p. 144. Sidney's relations with such scholars and printers as Philippus and Joachim Camerarius, Hubert Languet, Andreas Wechel, Henricus Stephanus, and others are described by McMahon, "Sidney's Letter to the Camerarii," *loc. cit.*, pp. 90 ff.

[34] McMahon, "Sidney's Letter to the Camerarii," *loc. cit.*, p. 92.

[35] Wallace, *op. cit.*, p. 183.

[36] These denunciations are almost identical with those made by Johann Stigel, pupil of Melancthon, in the Latin marriage hymn for Henry VIII and Anne of Cleves, preserved in *Poemata ex Recensione Adami Siberi* (Jena, 1577), II, 337–51, in the Johns Hopkins Library. Stigel and Melancthon, too, hoped for a Protestant league of princes, who would put out of their realms all the priests who "stir up dying quarrels and incite rulers to disagree and to wage savage wars." The Council of Trent, 1545–63, removed many of the causes for the Protestant revolt from the Church of Rome, but the remaining antagonisms and the evils described by Spenser were enough to bring on the terrible Thirty Years' War and the subsequent decline of Protestantism throughout Europe.

to heaven; who "boast they han the devill at commaund," but who have paid a pretty price, namely, their souls, for their alliance with him—all this would come better, certainly, from a well-informed layman like Sidney than from a parish rector like Greenham, who had not traveled enough to make such sweeping denunciations and whose aim was peace, not controversy; it would also be more characteristic of a world figure like Sidney than of a Welsh bishop like Richard Davies, whose own record was "not beyond reproach" though it was his business to combat such evils. Sidney, like Diggon, was also able to tell why the people everywhere complained of loss of faith because of "beastly and blont [that is, uncultivated]" clergy, who "casten too much of worlds care, to deck her [that is, their] heyre"; who, to provide rich livings for their families, so sorely taxed the people that "fewe chymneis reeking you shall espye," while the fat ox that used to lie in the poor man's stall is now secure in the clergy's purse. From his knowledge of the rich and powerful laity, Sidney was also able to denounce the rapacity of rulers and courtiers, who, like "bigge Bulles of Basan," encompassed the clergy about and "licked the fat from their beards," while the "leane soules" they trod under foot. It is folly, says Diggon, for the oppressed to complain, for they get nothing thereby, but only lose more. Hobbinoll's advice to "cleanly cover that cannot be cured," and his scolding of Diggon for saying there are any Wolves (Catholics) left in England where only Foxes (uncertain Anglicans like Elizabeth and Burghley) remain, give the final satiric touch to a very frank criticism of the Church in England and on the Continent in the 1570's.[37] Diggon is not so easily silenced, however, and he relates the story of Roffy and his dog Lowder, set upon by

[37] Some interesting evidence of Sidney's actual denunciation of the "wolves" in England and of his reporting concerning "the ingenious methods by which England was freed of wolves" was recorded by his friend Philippus Camerarius, (McMahon, "Sidney's Letter to the Camerarii," loc. cit., pp. 92–93). The evidence is recorded in Camerarius' book of Operae Horarum Succisivarum sive Meditationes Historicae, in which he states his admiration for Sidney as a man and recollects a conversation he had with him concerning the death of Sir Thomas More and religious conditions in England and Ireland, a conversation that probably took place in Prague, on Sidney's second visit to the Continent in 1577. If Sidney talked abroad of such English "wolves," there is every likelihood that he did so to his friends at home as well.

a "wicked Wolfe," proving that wolves were still secretly prowling about, two by two, in sheep's clothing, for fear of the laws against them.[38] Evidently Bishop Young of Rochester, the Roffy of the story, had had his own experience with prowlers in his fold and had saved his watchdog and his flock in the nick of time.[39] Since Bishop Young's diocese included Sidney's home parish of Penshurst, who—unless it be Spenser himself, as secretary of Bishop Young —would know better than Sidney what was going on there?

Perhaps the best recommendation for identifying Diggon as Sidney is that it makes much more understandable this dialogue between Harvey and his returned friend about the state of the Church abroad and at home. One's common sense is satisfied, and

[38] Lines 141–70 no doubt refer, as Professor Greenlaw suggests, *PMLA*, XXVI (1911), 437, and *Studies in Philology*, XI (1913), 22–23, to the Douai seminary priests, who came to England as missionaries of Catholicism. English Catholic exiles, saddened by the decline of Catholicism in England, founded a seminary for such missionaries in Douai in 1568. In 1577, one of them, Cuthbert Mayne, was executed, supposedly for bringing in a copy of a Papal Bull, but actually for preaching that Catholics would be justified in aiding a foreign army sent to restore England to the Church of Rome. Burghley, too, became alarmed and wrote to Elizabeth on January 28, 1580. Spenser's warning, according to Professor Greenlaw, was not so much due to his Puritan sympathies as to his knowledge "that these seminary priests, under their disguise as workmen, preached treason."

[39] F. M. Padelford, "Spenser and the Puritan Propaganda," *Modern Philology*, XI (1913), 100, says that the fable is "clearly based upon some trouble between Bishop Young and an aggressive Roman Catholic. Just what it was, we cannot say, but in view of the fact that Thomas Watson, the 'chief superior of the English Catholic clergy,' the very heart of the papal cause in England, was transferred to the keeping of the Bishop of Rochester at the request of the Bishop of Winchester, who had been burdened with the custody of Watson for five years, I think it not unlikely that the episode in some way relates to him." It was this same Dr. Watson who, like Sidney, was one of the entourage of the Earl of Lincoln in his journey abroad in 1572 and took seventeen-year-old Sidney to Germany for safety at the time of the St. Bartholomew's Massacre. In 1577, when Sidney again visited the Continent, Dr. Watson, now English ambassador at Brussels, wrote to Walsingham that Sidney had lodged with him there. (Cf. McMahon, "Sidney's Letter to the Camerarii," *loc. cit.*, p. 92) Watson had been Catholic Bishop of Lincoln under Mary. He was a cultured Cambridge humanist of Cheke's group and a friend of Ascham. He remained loyal to his Catholic faith through hardships and imprisonment. Though sixty-four in 1577, he was still suspected of under-cover proselytizing. Emile Legouis, *Edmund Spenser* (Paris, 1923), pp. 41–43, also implies that the Wolf in Spenser's story may have been Watson and that Spenser himself may be Lowder, saved by his master at a time when he was turning a too agreeable ear to the arguments of the old Catholic prelate. No doubt for Sidney himself, in his earlier association with Watson, such a story would have had a subtle warning.

hence one's appreciation of Spenser's purpose is enhanced. One or two lines may seem to cause the reader a little trouble, but can be explained, I think, without much difficulty. If some clerical import is seen in lines eight and nine:

> Where is the Fayre flocke, thou wast wont to leade?
> Or bene they chaffred? or at mischiefe dead?

one may find further reason for Sidney's being Diggon Davie in the fact that as a mere boy of nine he was assigned two benefices, one in Kent and one in Wales, and that later, "at some undetermined period," Elizabeth granted him another "Welsh sinecure [his father was Lord President of Wales] [40] worth £120 per annum." [41] "We shall probably not be far wrong," says Professor Wallace, "in assuming that throughout his life Philip Sidney's slender purse was chiefly replenished with moneys derived from his various benefices." [42] There was much buying and selling of benefices, as a form of revenue, in England as well as France, and the public conscience was not yet awake to the evils of such transactions. The Earl of Leicester was apparently engaged in the traffic, and in his will he authorized sale of "the parsonage of Warrington which I have in Lancashire." [43] Camden's *Annals* record the fact that most of Burghley's large holdings were "wrung by way of inequitable exchange from the church." [44] Sidney, or Diggon Davie, might therefore be asked, "Where is your fair flock . . . has it been sold?" Diggon's reply seems to indicate that his conscience has suffered in the matter, partly through the evils that he has seen abroad, for he says:

> Ah for love of that (which) is to thee moste leefe,
> Hobbinol, I pray thee gall not my old griefe:
> Sike question ripeth up cause of newe woe,

[40] Any evidence of western or Welsh dialect in the speeches of Diggon Davie would thus fit Sidney as well as Bishop Davies.

[41] Wallace, *op. cit.*, pp. 28–34.       [42] *Ibid.*, p. 34.

[43] Arthur Collins, *Letters and Memorials of State . . . written and collected by Sir Henry Sidney . . . the famous Sir Philip Sidney, etc.*, (London: printed for T. Osborne, 1746), I, 72.       [44] Grosart ed., I, 87.

and he proceeds to tell of how he went abroad in hope of other riches, but found none. In other words, why must Hobbinoll remind him of a practice of which he is ashamed?

In the following lines, Hobbinoll's assertion that he has not seen Diggon for "thrise three Moones," since which time Diggon has covered much ground, traveling "about the world rounde," may seem to present another difficulty, but the difficulty, I believe, is not a real one. The nine months cannot refer to the length of Sidney's stay abroad, since his first sojourn lasted almost three years and his second visit, which he made as ambassador of the Queen, covered about three months. Hobbinoll's statement, therefore, may simply mean that he has not seen Sidney for nine months, three months of which Sidney has spent abroad. One is reminded again of Sidney's inquiry about Harvey, reported in Spenser's letter to Harvey, whom Sidney says he has not seen.

If Diggon Davie is Sidney—and it seems most likely that he is—he had at least one chance to speak boldly and honestly, under cover of the New Poet's pastoral, concerning the vacillating policy of Elizabeth and Burghley in Church matters and concerning the fear of the return of Catholicism, which was already evident on the Continent. Only seven years later Sidney was to lose his life in Flushing, as leader in England's efforts to aid Continental Protestantism, and only thirty-five years later all of Europe was embroiled in the thirty years' struggle for the survival of Protestantism.

# MELANCTHON, STIGEL, AND HENRY VIII

THE MEDIEVAL theory of the divine origin of kingship—though weakened in England, as elsewhere, by the questioning of such republicans as Marsilius of Padua, William of Ockham, and Nicholas of Cusa; by historical events such as the deposition of Richard II, the election by parliament of Henry IV, and the subsequent Wars of the Roses; and by the impact of such early sixteenth-century theories as that the oldest estate was not the nobility, but the commons, and that from the ranks of labor came all other classes—remained, nevertheless, an important part of early sixteenth-century political theory and furnished both Tudors and Stuarts with a basis for the development of a strong monarchy and for the death blow to feudalism. Numerous English writers, both in prose and in verse, helped to keep the theory alive in the sixteenth century. To Edmund Dudley, Alexander Barclay, Thomas Elyot, John Cheke, Thomas Starkey, David Lyndsay, Robert Crowley, George Gascoigne, the authors of the *Mirrour for Magistrates* and the *Complaynt of Scotlande,* Thomas Dekker, Richard Hooker, and others, the theory of divine right was as real as it was to their predecessors in the Middle Ages.[1] It is important to note, however, that whereas on the Continent the theory remained largely one of royal absolutism and sovereignty, whereby the king was lawmaker and therefore above the law while nonresistance and obedience were enjoined by God on his subjects, the theory in England, in the sixteenth century as in the fifteenth, stressed the king's duty to rule with parliament, his subordination to law, both natural and positive, and his moral responsibility toward his subjects except in the spiritual realm where the duties of the clergy began.[2]

[1] I have discussed their treatment of the theme in *The Three Estates in Medieval and Renaissance Literature* (New York: Columbia University Press, 1933), pp. 143–229, 276–83.

[2] Cf. Franklin Le V. Baumer, *The Early Tudor Theory of Kingship* (New Haven:

A Saxon poet who is today all but forgotten, but whose influence
in the perpetuation of the divine right theory was considerable, was
Johannes Stigel, pupil of Melancthon and one of an embassy of
two sent in 1539 by Elector John Frederick of Saxony to Henry VIII
to promise Anne of Cleves, sister-in-law of John Frederick, as
Henry's fourth bride. Poets, in modern times, are not usually asked
to go on diplomatic missions, with instructions to achieve the aim
of the embassy by means of pleasing verses. Stigel's assignment,
however, seems to have been just that; and the poems surviving [3]
shed light on an interesting episode in the literary and political
relations of England and Germany in the latter half of Henry's
reign. Since Stigel was, for the most part, an occasional poet, cele-
brating persons famous in literature or history, his poems give a
fine insight into the times.

The situation in Protestant Germany and Protestant England
in 1539 made it seem desirable that some compact be achieved between them, for political as well as religious reasons.[4] In 1534
Henry VIII had acquired, by act of parliament, the title of "on earth
supreme head of the Church of England," thus severing the Church
of England from the Church of Rome and thus substituting for
the Catholic principle of a universal faith and a universal church
the principle of territorial religion, whereby each ruler or his people
could decide the faith to which they should adhere. Similarly the

---

Yale University Press, 1940), chap. v, "The King and the Law." As Dr. Baumer points
out (pp. 120 ff.), some historians, such as Figgis, Maitland, and others, maintain that
Tudor political theorists, like Continental writers, gave the king unlimited sovereignty, secular as well as spiritual. Such books as Tyndale's *Obedience of a Christian
Man* and Gardiner's *De Vera Obedientia*, however, make no such claims, but favor
a "mixed government," with the king ruling in conjunction with parliament. In 1558
Christopher Goodman's *How Superior Powers Ought to Be Obeyed* was the beginning
of a series of important political writings that marked a definite departure from the
doctrines of nonresistance of the first half of the century.

[3] They are in *Delitiae Poetarum Germanorum huius superiorisque aevi illustrium*, ed.
Jan Gruter (Frankfort, 1612), Part VI, pp. 559-62, a copy of which is in the Columbia
University Library, and in *Poemata ex Recensione Adami Siberi* (Jena, 1577), II, 337-
51, which is in the Johns Hopkins Library, probably the only copy in America. An
eight-volume edition of Stigel's verse, which I have not seen, appeared in Jena in 1566.

[4] John Richard Green, *History of the English People* (New York: Macmillan
Company, 1882), II, 181.

Lutheran princes of north Germany repudiated Rome for the purpose of freedom of worship within their own domains; and, much
as he disliked Lutheranism, Henry offered them his alliance, against
Emperor Charles V. It was the desire of Henry's secretary and Vicar-
General, Thomas Cromwell, that the alliance with the German
princes be cemented by marriage, and so it was that the Elector
of Saxony, urged on perhaps by the Scotch pupil of Melancthon,
Alexander Alesius,[5] sent Francis Burchart, professor of Greek at
Wittenberg and later one of the diplomatic corps of Saxony, ac-
companied by Stigel, to England to arrange for the marriage. The
story of Henry's marriage to Anne in January, 1540, his strong
aversion to her, his rebellion against Cromwell, his divorce on
July 9, 1540, and the death of Cromwell on the scaffold in the same
month is a familiar one. Had the alliance endured, it might have
changed all Europe and averted the terrible Thirty Years' War.[6]
Nothing, however, turned out as Cromwell had planned. Later,
when it was clear that Rome was not to yield but was growing
more powerful throughout Europe, Henry tried again, in the last
months of his life, to offer aid to the League of Schmalkald, but
his offer came too late, and his help was rejected.

Nevertheless, in 1539 hopes ran high on both sides of the Channel.
Stigel's faith in the union of Henry and Anne was shared by most
of his Lutheran countrymen. As a student in the University of
Wittenberg, Stigel had won the esteem and affection of both
Melancthon and Luther, as well as that of the group of gifted
young writers to which he belonged. Melancthon, seeking to stimu-
late the writing of poetry, was drawn to Stigel as the most promising
member of the group.[7] It was Melancthon who urged Stigel to
write; it was through the recommendation of Melancthon that
Stigel became professor of Latin at Wittenberg and later professor of
classical languages at the University of Jena; it was with Melancthon's

---

[5] Karl Wilhelm Goettling, *Vita Johannes Stigelii Thuringi* (Jena, 1858), p. 38.

[6] Green, *op. cit.*, II, 191.

[7] Georg Ellinger, "Johannes Stigel als Lyriker: Ein Beitrag zur Geschichte der neu-
lateinischen Dichtung," *Neue Jahrbücher für das Klassische Altertum, Geschichte und
deutsche Literatur für Pädagogik*, XXXIX (Leipzig, 1917), 374–98.

encouragement that Stigel, in 1539, went to England and wrote his poems about his visit and an Epithalamium about the marriage that followed; it was Melancthon who, in September, 1540, in one of his ninety-six letters to Stigel [8] called him *Elegantissimi ingenii poeta* but warned him against writing any more poems in praise of Henry VIII; it was Melancthon to whom Stigel wrote some of his best occasional verse, full of profound admiration for that great humanist, who helped to guide Protestant Germany in the turmoil of its conflict with Rome. At Jena he wrote in honor of many important persons of the day, including Luther, the Elector of Saxony, and Emperor Charles V, who named him Poet Laureate. At his death Stigel was celebrated in Latin epitaphs as a second Eobanus Hessus. His own modest epitaph he wrote as follows:

> Hic ego Stigelius iaceo; quis curat? ut omnis
> Negligat hoc mundus, scit tamen ipse deus.[9]

The short poems that Stigel wrote on the occasion of his visit to England express a warm admiration for England and the English and Henry VIII.[10] An "Epigram in Arcem Regis Angliae, cui nomen Hampthencurt" asks why his friends have never told him of the beauties of Hampton Court. One would need a thousand eyes to see all its beauties. "Let the golden house of magnificent Nero and the great palace of Caius Caesar yield to it! as their homes surpassed those of cultured Rome, so this home surpasses the elegance of Europe." [11] Another epigram on the same theme says: "I do not know how much credibility must be given to your theaters, O Rome; what I see almost makes me ashamed to believe. To such an extent, even beyond all natural capacity and art, do we attempt to build heavenly homes in the midst of the country. Whoever sees these monuments of the King of Britain marvels that human hands could build such things." Similarly he admires "the blue waters of the Thames" and the swans there, "singing

---

[8] Preserved in the *Corpus Reformatorum*, ed. C. G. Bretschneider, (Halle, 1836–42), Vols. III to IX.    [9] Goettling, *op. cit.*, p. 38.
[10] *Delitiae Poetarum Germanorum*, pp. 559–62.    [11] *Ibid.*, p. 561.

sweet songs of their fatherland." He calls upon the "Glorious King" to regard the priests of Apollo, "since he [Apollo] denies nothing in all Parnassus" to King Henry.[12] The "form and modest manners" of many a girl in London are pleasing to Stigel. When he is asked why he marries none of them, however, he reminds himself that one must know more about a woman than her appearance to wed her.[13] In five epigrams "De Regina Angliae Anna" [14] Stigel speaks of the beauty and virtue of Anne of Cleves in the more general terms of the later Epithalamium.

It is in the Epithalamium,[15] a poem of 744 lines, that Stigel has an opportunity to set forth his theories of kingship at some length. The title assigned the poem in the 1566 edition of Stigel's poems is "De ordinatione magistratus et subditorum elegia," showing that its philosophic import is of even more significance than the occasion which called it forth. The hymn may be divided into eleven general parts: (1) the poet's appeal to Piety, instead of Venus, for aid, 58 lines; (2) praise of Henry and Anne and their proposed union, 29 lines; (3) the story of Eve's unlike children, 226 lines; (4) the shameful state of the Catholic Church, 62 lines; (5) the duty of a king: to defend true religion, 102 lines; (6) the teachings of true religion, 26 lines; (7) future renown of Henry as defender of the faith, 16 lines; (8) description of the embarkation of Anne for England, 118 lines; (9) praise of Anne and good wishes for her future, 9 lines; (10) praise of England and Henry, 7 lines; (11) Stigel's disillusionment and retraction of his praise, 91 lines.

The purpose of the hymn is evident in the opening invocation to Piety. It is she, not Venus, who presides over marriages ordained by God. In the marriage of Anne and Henry, God promises a fortunate destiny, for Anne is distinguished by all virtues, and Henry is a king rich in all the attributes that make kings closest to God. God commands regard from all mortals, but He expects it first from kings, those who give laws to others and who ought to institute righteous laws and be an example to all devout people.

---

[12] *Ibid.*  [13] *Ibid.*, p. 559.  [14] *Ibid.*, pp. 560, 561, 562.
[15] *Poemata ex Recensione Adami Siberi*, II, 337 ff.

In enforcing his sermonlike theme, Stigel finds the story of Eve's unlike children very useful. Almost a third of the poem is devoted to it. The story, familiar in both England and Germany in the sixteenth century,[16] explains kingship as a direct ordination by God of the noblest of Eve's children for the sake of peace and harmony in the world. God, on His visit to Eve, consecrates the peace-loving, worshipful Abel and Seth as kings, to rule over the rest. Theirs, says Stigel, is a holy duty: to make clear the splendor of faith and true reverence and honor to God; to give rights and laws; to defend the borders of the fatherland; to punish the evil; and to bless the good with peace:

> Vestrum erit acceptum fidei illustrare nitorem,
> Et verum cultum, noticiamque Dei.
> Iura dare, ac leges, patriae defendere fines,
> Poena arcere malos, pace fovere bonos.[17]

Cain, on the other hand, is churlish and grumbling; he therefore becomes ancestor of all those who labor. It is their duty to fear and obey the laws and to endure servitude and to know that the rule of kings is the word of God:

> At Cain impatiens, & qui nascentur ab illo,
> Agnatae haeredes rusticitatis erunt.
> Horum munus erit parare, ac iura timere,
> Et vestras leges, servitiumque pati:
> Atque opera vestra divinum agnoscere verbum.[18]

This division of classes and duties is the only one made by Stigel; all other orders of society are ignored. Even those who maintain the teaching of true doctrine, usually the clergy, are here identified as those who rule, as Henry and the German Lutheran princes

[16] Cf. Johannes Winzer, *Die Ungleichen Kinder Evas in der Literatur des Sechszehnten Jahrhunderts* (Greifswald: F. W. Kunike, 1908). The author discusses some seventeen folk versions, from the Mohammedan to the Scandinavian countries and Wales, including its use by Mantuan, Melancthon, Sixt Bircks, and Hans Sachs. He omits, however, Alexander Barclay's English version of it in his fifth eclogue of *Certain Eclogues*, which I have discussed in *The Three Estates in Medieval and Renaissance Literature*, p. 149.

[17] Page 343, ll. 23–26.          [18] Page 343, ll. 27–31.

believed they should be. The importance of such division of duties
is stressed at some length, just as it is in numerous sixteenth-century
discussions of the same theme. If there is to be peace and harmony
in the world, says Stigel, there must be kings to command and
subjects to obey. Only God can provide true leaders for his people
—leaders who will make just laws and enforce them. Even Eve,
among her numerous children, found some unruly; and it was to
restore order among them that God instituted rulers.

The rest of the hymn, often in vivid phrases, describes the state
of the pre-Reformation Church on the Continent and stresses the
great need of Henry VIII's defense of the true faith, namely, Protestantism. This, says Stigel, can be best achieved by Henry's union
with Anne. It was Pope Leo X who, in 1521, had conferred the
title of Defender of the Faith on Henry; and it was Stigel's purpose
to insure Henry's right to it by his defense of Protestantism. The
Church, Stigel says, is weeping over its sad state. Priests of corrupt
Rome are full of deceit. Instead of teaching the words of God,
they become vehement tyrants, dry-throated in their zeal, and they
goad dying quarrels with spurs and incite leaders in disagreement
to savage wars:

> Esse sacerdotes habitu fallente putabit,
>   Qui cupiant summi verba docere Dei:
> Non sunt: sed sicca flagrantes fauce Tyranni,
>   Qui cupiant ipsi bella movere Deo:
> Qui stimulis agitant animos, litesque serentes,
>   Unanimes actiunt ad fera bella duces.[19]

[19] Page 344, ll. 5–10. The charges made by Stigel against the Church are, as I have
pointed out above, p. 26, n. 36, remarkable in their similarity to those in Spenser's
*Shepheardes Calender*, especially the September eclogue, lines 80–87:

> For eyther the shepeheards bene ydle and still,
> And ledde of theyr sheepe, what way they wyll:
> Or they bene false, and full of covetise,
> And casten to compasse many wrong emprise.
> But the more bene fraight with fraud and spight,
> Ne in good nor goodnes taken delight:
> But kindle coales of conteck and yre,
> Wherewith they sette all the world on fire.

The Church has long lain bound in the strong chains of these tyrants. They suck up its blood and tear its viscera. Now they hire mercenaries to fight their battles; mercenaries who, for gold, seek out foes by arousing madness when there is no foe of whom to complain. They rage through the halls of kings, destroying all peace and order. The name of priest should be honored, but now shameful and unlawful things are done in that name.[20] There are well-known immoralities among them, which alone should enrage the minds of kings. In the marriage of Henry and Anne, however, the Church finds cause for rejoicing, for here is a king with strength so great that printed word can scarcely tell of it adequately. Therefore, let this great king defend the cause of true religion. His piety has long been known in all lands; other rulers know that true religion is his cause. By his example he will inspire the rest. The hopes of all the people are with him. Alas, why do plagues and priests and false teachers (mystics) delay him? Henry is urged to drive the priests out from his country's assembly and purge his tables of their poisonous presence.[21]

Stigel's theories of monarchy are most clearly stated in his effort to enforce the idea that it is Henry VIII's duty to defend the true faith. The king, he says, is the state, that he may serve the public need. The public need is that of the people, namely, the Word of God. God commands kings to defend His Word. This one peculiar duty He commands of kings. Thence kings are called sacred and the care of Heaven. The king is unworthy of his title who denies his duty. The Church received kings as sent by Heaven, as those whom God gives to defend true doctrine. Kings are given great minds, both to move ignorant hearts and to turn the learned

[20] The Council of Trent, 1545–63, removed many of the causes for these charges of profligacy and dishonesty against Popes and clergy; the Popes, at least, became as moral as Luther or Calvin. However, the antagonisms and some of the evils remained, as Spenser's *Shepheardes Calender* of 1579 shows.

[21] The same wish is expressed for Elizabeth's reign in the September eclogue of Spenser's *Shepheardes Calender*, except that there the priests (referred to as "wolves") are no longer found in council chambers, but, disguised as sheep, have kept their places in the Church.

against evil. A king who wastes such gifts from Heaven suffers punishment for his irreverence:

> Publica res rex est, ut publica commoda dervet.
>   Publica sunt populi commoda, verba Dei.
> Regibus haec mandat Deus ut tueantur, id unum
>   Officium proprium regibus esse iubet.
> Inde sacri reges & coeli cura vocantur.
>   Indignus titulo est, qui negat ista, suo.
> Accipit a coelo missos Ecclesia reges,
>   Quos dat, ut adservent dogmata vera, Deus.
> Hinc vobis animi ingentes, & nescia frangi
>   Pectora, & adversum vincere docta malum.
> Muneribus coeli iam si quis abutitur illis;
>   Pro tanta poenas impietate luit.[22]

The false teachings of Rome steal from God His just honors. Pretending to be God Himself, the Roman Baal makes men buy the realms of their native Heaven, whereas God promises them free. Images, incense, purgatory, forgiveness of sins by the priest, the sale of salvation for money—such lies the tyranny of the priests fashioned. Now Henry knows these vain abuses of the devil and deceptions of the priests. He knows that he is begotten from the seed of Abel, to preserve true doctrine. True doctrine Stigel defines as: that which teaches the cross and salvation by Christ's mercy and atonement. Henry's reward as Defender of the Faith will be great in Heaven and among his posterity on earth. A golden statue with noble inscriptions will perpetuate his fame. He will be renowned as the Prince who joined France and Protestant Germany to England in a strong federation. Future generations will scatter roses in his tomb, and England will be dear to God Himself.

Such were Stigel's thoughts, he says, when one day, as a horseman in the retinue of Anne, he beheld the royal pomp of her embarkation for England. The vivid description of opening harbor gates,

[22] Page 345, l. 47, to p. 346, l. 2.

of rejoicing throngs, of wild applause, of machines hurling fire-
works of "sulphurous acorn-shaped balls of lead like lightning-bolts
up to highest Heaven," of the dense smoke that followed, of the
clangor of trumpets and roll of drums, of noblemen on horses
wheeling in graceful circles, of the fair and honorable Anne drawn
in a golden carriage, of the royal insignia on painted sails, of sailors
on the highest masts singing out their hopes of a calm journey—all
this makes Stigel's reference to Cleopatra and her gilded ships on
the River Cydnus seem pale by comparison. Such was undoubtedly
his desire.

The hymn closes with Stigel's final praise of Henry and Anne
and his hopes for their future. As, in his imagination, he sees the
shores of Kent reaching out to meet the ship, he exclaims, O happy
England, receive this gift to your calm land. He is reminded of
the Saxon blood that gave England its propitious beginnings and
that now is to form a new bond between them.

It was to this ardent plea for Henry's aid in support of Protestantism that Stigel was later forced to add his retraction, a palinode
full of profound regret and moving in its expression of his strong
feeling. Abruptly he speaks of the forlorn hope of many in the
justice of the King of England. The English Church had looked
for better days, but all in vain. He shudders now at the thought of
the fierce poisons of Roman deceit. Is he to be accused of having
sung the praises of a tyrant? Strangely enough, at this point Stigel
seems still to hope that the rumors of Henry's tyranny may be
false, that he will not be deceived by the abominable undertakings
of the priests, that he may still be Aeneas for Stigel's verse. However,
on August 17, 1540, Melancthon, in a letter to Stigel, curtly summed
up the reasons why German poets should write no more verses
in praise of Henry VIII. "Let us stop sounding the praises of the
English Nero," he wrote.

I do not know whether you have heard about his cruelty to the
Queen. If you know anything about the matter, you can easily
understand with what feelings our people will read those eulogies.

. . . I will change my preface to general matters and will add an ode retracting the praise, even though it is not very abundant. Cromwell has been strangled in a noose; he has been quartered and burned.[23]

Thus ended Stigel's praise of Henry VIII. As a descendant of Abel, consecrated by God to the duty of defending the Protestant cause, Henry had proved unworthy. Stigel's plea for an international responsibility in the preservation of true doctrine had failed, just as Cromwell's plans for an alliance by marriage had failed. Moreover, Stigel's theories of kingship, though held by many on the Continent, were too far-reaching for Tudor use. Fortunately for England and for the Continent and for the world, the English Reformation proceeded without the aid of royal absolutism, though Tudor faith in the divine origin of kingship helped to establish a monarchy strong enough to cope with the rivalries of feudal barons. Meanwhile on the Continent the power of the Elector of Saxony and his Protestant cause declined, and the way was prepared for the Thirty Years' War. Stigel outlived Henry and saw the reign of Catholic Mary give way to that of Protestant Elizabeth. In 1562, at the time of his death, when English Protestantism seemed established, the theory of the divine origin of kings was also scarcely questioned; it remained for the Stuarts and Hobbes to assert the unlimited sovereignty that had seemed so sound to Stigel, but that the English finally destroyed by means of civil war. Nevertheless, in its stress on unity and authority and respect for the law, the theory of divine ordination of kings served the needs of the time well. As a target for attack by seventeenth-century defenders of liberty, it was also useful, for by that time nothing was so clear as its fallacies.

[23] Latin text quoted by Goettling, *op. cit.*, p. 16, from the *Corpus Reformatorum*.

# THEORIES OF MONARCHY IN "MUM AND THE SOTHSEGGER"

THE LITERATURE of the estates of the world, so clearly developed in medieval France and England, was further enriched for the modern reader by the publication in 1936 of the fifteenth-century satire *Mum and the Sothsegger*.[1] Discovered in the west country, near the locale of *Piers Plowman*, to which it bears a number of similarities, it reviews the condition of "all kinds of estates," [2] from king to peasant, in the eventful last days of Richard II and the early years of the reign of Henry IV. Though a part of the newly discovered manuscript is a fragment of alliterative verse already published [3] under the title *Richard the Redeles*, the much larger part concerning the case of Mum and the Truthteller was unknown to modern readers and seems to have been largely neglected since its publication. The question of the relation of the two fragments is unsettled; but since in the sixteenth century they were known as one poem under the title of *Mum, Sothsegger*, since their language and form are identical, and since certain ideas in the two parts are closely related,[4] there is good reason for considering them here together as parts of a single poem.

Many of the characteristics of the literature of estates as they are to be found in other works of this type are also found in *Mum and the Sothsegger*. Its classification of all society, its stress on the necessity of the three estates and on the duties of each to the others to maintain a stable realm, its indication of the faults of each class, its doctrine

---

[1] Eds. Mabel Day and Robert Steele, *E.E.T.S.*, orig. ser., 199 (London: Oxford University Press, 1936).

[2] "Alle maniere estatz," p. 50, l. 793.

[3] Twice by Thomas Wright and later, in 1873, by W. W. Skeat. It was Skeat's theory that the poem was unquestionably written by the author of *Piers Plowman*, Langland, but Thomas Wright said it was not by Langland.

[4] See editors' Intro., pp. xviii–xix.

of love as the remedy for their shortcomings, and its use of such familiar devices as the débat, the dream vision allegory, and the narrative of journeying in search of information are all familiar from other works of the same tradition. The purpose of the author in writing, however, was not simply that of following his predecessors in a more or less stereotyped literary pattern of enumeration and lament. He had a duty to perform for his king: that of advising him as to the nature of true monarchy, the advantages of monarchy, the authority by which monarchy stood, and the fate of monarchy if it failed in its duty of upholding the law and thus maintaining justice and peace. Since, before the book was completed, Richard II (king by the law of primogeniture) was deposed, and Henry IV (king by act of Parliament) had ascended the throne, the whole problem of kingship became one of extreme importance and one about which the new king needed advice as much as his predecessor, if not more. Though Henry had been hailed as a kind of savior of the realm, the evils of Richard's reign went unredressed, and added to the evils was a new kind of secrecy, that meant flattery at court and eavesdropping on the commons. Those who spoke the truth were soon put in prison, and some were put to death. In 1401 the Statute *De Haeretico Comburendo* was passed, to deal with those who spoke against the Church, and Lollard persecution increased. Therefore, though the author of *Mum and the Sothsegger* had begun his book boldly, with an occasional bit of beast or bird allegory, all pretty obvious to those at court, he proceeded with more caution, under cover of pretended ignorance, to a narrative of a ten-year search for truth among all the estates of the realm, and a more extended dream vision allegory. The political theory of the author did not change, however, with the change of kings. No doubt the deposition and death of Richard and the presence of the much-lauded Bolingbroke on the throne only strengthened his faith in his doctrine concerning kingship in general. In the latter, more cautious part of his book he adds the very lively and significant theme, derived from the words of Christ himself and supported by both classical and medieval authority, that he who is silent about the evils of the realm consents to them and is as guilty as the doer; but this addition, likewise, has no effect on his political doctrine, and is, in fact, a clever means of justifying his earlier boldness as well as his later more guarded, but no less pointed, criticism.

What, then, were the chief theories of monarchy as set forth by this philosopher-poet in the late fourteenth century and early fifteenth century, at a time so significant for the future political history of England? Was he, in the light of political theory of his own day, a conservative or a liberal? To what other medieval political theorists was he most nearly related? And from what evidence did he and his contemporaries or predecessors derive their conclusions? Needless to say, the study of these fourteenth- and fifteenth-century theories of monarchy sheds light on all succeeding theory; and the student of sixteenth- and seventeenth-century political literature is hard pressed to understand the problems of tenure and divine right in those times without some understanding of the chief political theories of the Middle Ages.

Had *Mum and the Sothsegger* been written in the thirteenth or early fourteenth century, it might have had something to say of the conflicts between Papacy and Empire and between Empire and National Monarchy. In those times the genuinely medieval theorist, imbued with the medieval passion for unity, began with a single God-State, divinely founded and comprising every human community, whether village, city, province, or kingdom, in a kind of federalistic system.[5] To Dante,[6] as to John of Salisbury [7] and others, the term *monarchy* meant a single world empire, and the monarch or *princeps* was emperor, not king. By the end of the fourteenth

[5] Otto von Gierke, *Political Theories of the Middle Age,* transl. with Intro. by Frederic W. Maitland (Cambridge [Eng.]: University Press, 1900), pp. 20–21. Cf. also R. W. and A. J. Carlyle, *A History of Medieval Political Theory in the West* (Edinburgh and London: Wm. Blackwood & Sons, 1903–36), III, 170–80, and V, 141–49; also William A. Dunning, *A History of Political Theories Ancient and Medieval* (New York: Macmillan Company, 1935), pp. 230 ff.

[6] *De Monarchia,* ed. Dr. E. Moore (Oxford: Clarendon Press, 1916), p. 344: "Et sic omnes partes praenotatae infra regna et ipsa regna ordinari debent ad unum Principem, sive Principatum, hoc est, ad Monarcham, sive Monarchiam."

[7] *Polycraticus,* ed. Clemens C. I. Webb (Oxford: Clarendon Press, 1909), I, 235: "Est ergo, ut eum plerique diffiniunt, princeps potestas publica et in terris quaedam divinae maiestatis imago." Cf. James Brown Scott, *Law, the State, and the International Community* (New York: Columbia University Press, 1939), I, 206–12.

century, however, the decline of the power of Papacy and Empire and the growing power of national monarchies, accelerated by the doctrines of the ancients, marked the supremacy of the idea of nationalism, rather than imperialism, especially in England, France, and Spain. Consequently, the author of *Mum* has nothing to say of those larger aspects of medieval political theory, but confines his argument to the theories of national monarchy alone. He is a nationalist, caring little about the claims of Empire or Papacy. Writing after the time of such new and liberal thinkers as Marsilius of Padua and William of Ockham, he is, moreover, a nationalist whose faith, like theirs, is fixed in monarchy limited by a sovereignty of the people, evolved according to Natural Law and maintained by representation and by due process of law. Such earlier theorists as Thomas Aquinas [8] and Aegidius Colonna were favorable to national or even city monarchy, and to national monarchy limited by obligations of duty, but they would scarcely have understood the limitations imposed by the "decisively republican" [9] theorists of the later fourteenth and fifteenth centuries, as well as by the author of *Mum* in his book of government.[10] To Marsilius of Padua and to William of Ockham the need of a single head is also obvious, whether "regnum aut civitas" [11] is to be ruled justly; but their "principans" is only the enforcer of the law, and the law is made by the people, as we shall see later.

Though the author of *Mum* has no thought for the conflicts of Empire and Papacy, he is, like the theorists of his own day, fully aware of the problems involved in the institution of national monarchy if it is to survive. The conflicts of his own day are, briefly:

[8] *De Regimine Principum*, transl. Gerald B. Phelan (London and New York: Sheed and Ward, 1938), p. 39: "It is plain, therefore, from what has been said, that a king is one who rules the people of one city or province and rules them for the public good."

[9] Gierke, *op. cit.*, p. 46.

[10] See, however, the remarkable assertions of Manegold of Lautenbach, an eleventh-century Alsatian priest, in Reginald L. Poole's *Illustrations of the History of Medieval Learning* (London: Society for Promoting Christian Knowledge; New York: Macmillan Company, 1932), pp. 203–4.

[11] Marsilius of Padua, *Defensor Pacis*, ed. C. W. Previté-Orton (Cambridge [Eng.]: University Press, 1928), p. 89.

the doctrine of monarchy as opposed to that of feudalism; the doctrine of monarchy instituted by popular sovereignty and maintained by due process of law as opposed to lawless absolutism; the theory of passive obedience as opposed to that of resistance and even tyrannicide; and finally the distinctive and sometimes divergent claims of Positive and Natural Law.

In his consideration of these problems, the author of *Mum* is always the practical legist,. with one eye on theory and the other on the law and the courts. His emphasis on the law is everywhere apparent.[12] In that emphasis, as well as in his nationalism, especially as he applies it with deference to the ancients and their faith in law, always tested by the dictates of reason, he looks forward to the advent of the modern era rather than backward to medieval theories of divine ordination and divine right, incapable of legal limitation beyond the demands of Natural Law. Like the thirteenth-century English jurist Henry de Bracton, with whose *De Legibus et Consuetudinibus Angliae* he was no doubt familiar, he recognizes the reasonableness of Roman law, consciously revived in the University of Bologna and elsewhere in the twelfth century and taught at Oxford and Cambridge in spite of protests, such as those of Wycliffe,[13] that English customary law was superior and should not be supplanted by Roman or "Civil" Law as the folk laws of other nations had been supplanted on the Continent. The author of *Mum* in one instance cites Roman Law as a standard in his criticism of English case law.[14] However, also like Bracton, he is obviously most familiar with English case law, and in his listing of the faults of all estates as found in a bag full of books at the close of Fragment M, he seems to be writing with a lawyer's notebook or a group of plea rolls before

[12] In this respect, also, he is like Marsilius of Padua, whose "demonstration . . . is chiefly legal." C. W. Previté-Orton, "Marsilius of Padua," *Proceedings of the British Academy*, XXII (1935), 18. Cf. also Scott, *op. cit.*, I, 271–77.

[13] *Tractatus de Officio Regis*, ed. A. W. Pollard and Charles Sayle (London: Trübner & Co., 1887), pp. 189–93. Wycliffe's objections are that Roman Civil Law is an obstacle to theology, that all that is true in Roman Law is found in the Scriptures, that Roman Law permits many things contrary to religion. As for the argument that Roman Law is superior to English Law he says: "Sed non credo quod plus viget in Romana civilitate subtilitas racionis sive iusticia quam in civilitate Anglicana."

[14] Page 74, ll. 1619–20, 1624–25.

him. The reader of *Mum* is naturally prone to speculate as to whether the author may have been a member of one of the Inns of Court and perhaps also a member of Parliament, since he knows so much about the affairs of the realm. It was the medieval English schools of law, the Inns of Court, and the Yearbooks of recorded cases read in those schools that prevented the invasion of Roman law and preserved English common law, both in the Middle Ages and later in the days of the Stuarts.[15] It is possible that the author of *Mum* was one of those common lawyers who thus helped to preserve the traditions of liberty that are the glory of English common law and that we in America have inherited. Above all, however, as one who, like most medieval theorists, reveres the Gospel as the source of all law,[16] the author of *Mum* is aware, as we shall see later, of the primary authority of God's law or Natural Law in all cases and all courts.

Whether the author of *Mum* knew Aristotle and his *Politics* or any other political theory of the ancients at first hand is impossible to say, since he nowhere names any "learned" sources. However, the republicanism of Aristotle, familiar, like Roman Law, since the latter half of the twelfth century, gradually permeated medieval doctrine, and there is every reason to suppose that the author of *Mum* was aware of such theory, whether from ancient sources directly or from such theorists as William of Ockam and Marsilius of Padua, to whom, as to Aristotle, no one form of government was more "divine" than another. Nor is it strange that the author of *Mum* should espouse the ancient theory of the natural, rational evolution of law and government since, as an English legist, he knew that English case law had slowly evolved from English customary or common law, and that in no sense had it been the result of divine imposition or special dispensation. Thus he has little to say of government as *iure divino*, but treats it rather as the outgrowth of practical necessity and fitness and reason.

From his knowledge of law and of English politics past and

[15] "Common Law," *Encyclopedia Britannica*, 14th ed. (1937), VI, 123. For a discussion of "The Influence of Roman Law in England" see Scott, *op. cit.*, I, 252–64.

[16] Page 74, l. 1622.

present, the author of *Mum* has come to a firm belief in monarchy as the best form of national government, and in this, as we have seen, he is in accord with other medieval theorists.[17] His chief reason for such preference, however, is that it is the form best able to cope with feudalism. Everyone knows, he says, that "hit is holsum forto haue a heede of vs alle, That is a king y-corouned to kepe vs vnder lawe, To put vs into prisone when we passe boundes."[18] If there were no such head, the reckless lords would "renne on eche other."[19] Neither Richard II nor Henry IV had proved the real benefits of monarchy, for Richard was ruled by his feudal barons, the worst element among them, and Henry had trouble with his liege lords from the start. The essential doctrine of feudalism, that of the "infinite divisibility of sovereign power,"[20] had undermined the authority of the crown. "Full preuyly they pluckud / thy power awey,"[21] he asserts in his warning to Richard, until the crown was cracked,[22] the people alienated, and the realm in a state of complete disorder. Raising his voice, therefore, against what to him was the chief evil of the day, the author of *Mum* denounces again and again the encroachments of the lords on the power of the king. He blames Richard not only for permitting such encroachments, but also for encouraging them by his dispersal of crown rights and revenues among his barons, his putting his seal of authority upon them in the form of royal badges, and his sanction of their authority, even in courts of law. Henry IV is a man of virtues, and he has good councillors, but he is in danger of giving them too much power and also of dividing his revenues so that he has no funds for the things it is his duty to perform. Such favoring of one estate

[17] Cf. Gierke, *op. cit.*, pp. 30 ff. Though Wycliffe believes that the best form of government in theory is a rule by judges and by divine law alone, as in Old Testament days, he, too, says that in practice monarchy is best, for almost every reason: it is approved by God, by reason, and by philosophy; the Body Politic must have one Head; Aristotle thought monarchy best, and so did Ambrose, Augustine, and Gregory. *De Civili Dominio*, ed. Reginald L. Poole (London: Trübner & Company, 1885), pp. 192 ff., 205; also *Tractatus de Officio Regis*, ed. Pollard and Sayle, p. 246.

[18] Page 74, ll. 1630–33.          [19] Page 74, l. 1635.

[20] J. N. Figgis, *The Theory of the Divine Right of Kings* (2d ed.; Cambridge [Eng.]: University Press, 1934), p. 30.

[21] Page 5, l. 52.          [22] Page 5, l. 70.

of the realm to the exclusion of another causes grumbling and defection among the commons, who, if dealt with justly, according to the law, would love their king as subjects ought to do. That the author's fears of feudalism were not groundless was proved some fifty years later by the growing friction between Yorkists and Lancastrians and finally by the Wars of the Roses—a period of lawlessness and disorder that was resolved only when Tudor might was able to make of monarchy a power that was more than a match for ambitious barons.

In support of his faith in monarchy the author of *Mum* twice uses the figure of the Body Politic,[23] so familiar in medieval political doctrine, from that of John of Salisbury [24] in the twelfth century to its fullest use by Nicholas of Cusa [25] in the fifteenth century. The importance of the head to the body is naturally his theme in using this anthropomorphic comparison. By means of it he first stresses the ill effects suffered by all members of the body if the head is injured; and later he warns some of the commons, who are the hands of the body, of the danger to the head and to themselves in indiscriminate criticism of the king.

The doctrine of monarchy is also enforced by the author's use of a bit of medieval science, that of bee-keeping. In a dream vision he learns about the government of bees from a wise old gardener, who, in a sense, is also a symbol of good government, for he keeps his garden according to "the law," namely, that of destroying everything that injures it and protecting everything that is good. The bee, says the gardener, is the best governed of all creatures and is therefore a worthy teacher. Bees choose as king [26] one who is fit "by

[23] Page 49, ll. 763–64 and p. 69, l. 1472.

[24] *Polycraticus,* ed. Webb, Vol. V, chaps. vi, ix, x, xi; Vol. VI, chaps. i, xx, xxv.

[25] *Opera Omnia,* Vol. XIV, *Concordantia Catholica,* ed. Gerhardus Kallen (Leipzig: F. Meiner, 1939), Book I.

[26] The author of *Mum,* using Bartholomew the Englishman's *Bestiary* as his source, translates *rex* as "king" instead of "queen," apparently in a generic sense for "ruler." This argument for monarchy, as well as other arguments drawn from natural phenomena, is a common one. Cf. Thomas Aquinas, *De Regimine Principum,* transl. G. B. Phelan, pp. 40–42. In Shakespeare's *Henry V,* Act I, scene 2, ll. 187–204, the lesson of the bees is drawn again, and the bees' ruler is called a "king."

kinde" [27] to wear the crown. He is the most merciful and the gentlest of all of them. He rules by reason and just laws and by consent of all the rest.[28] This good king the rest all serve and obey and protect, princes and workers alike. Thus they live and work together, for the "comune profit" [29]—all but the drones, who are finally detected and killed. A wise tale, the author replies, with much meaning for whoever can meditate.

Similarly, in his defense of monarchy, the author turns, as did most medieval political theorists, to the aid of medieval history. There he finds the tale of Jhengiz Khan,[30] who, when asked to unite seven warring princes under a single head, did so to the benefit of all. To test their loyalty, "as cronicle of hym telleth," [31] he established two statutes: the first that they slay their eldest sons and heirs, and the second that they give to him all their lands forever; and they did his bidding. Then he called knights and others to a council, and they "wroughte alle with oon wil as wise men shuld," [32] and so prospered greatly. The rebellious estates of Henry's realm would do well to heed the lesson of unity and harmony as taught by Jhengiz Khan.

Had the author of *Mum* argued simply for national monarchy, as opposed to feudalism, there would be little to distinguish his theories from those of most medieval defenders of monarchy. Earlier theorists, as we have seen, agreed as to their preference for the rule of One Head, whether national or imperial, and they did so on the basis of God's approval, or from evidence from natural phenomena, or on the authority of the Scriptures, the Church Fathers, and the ancients, or from evidence found in the tales of medieval historians and scientists, or, in fact, on the basis of almost any source available.[33] To most of these earlier theorists, moreover, the monarch became

[27] Page 56, l. 999.          [28] Page 57, ll. 1036-37.
[29] Page 58, l. 1078. The reason for government is often discussed in medieval political theory. To John of Salisbury it is "aequitas" or "iustitia." To Marsilius of Padua it is "vita sufficiens." To William of Ockham it is, as here, the "utilitas communis." To Thomas Aquinas it is "unity," "order," "peace," "delight in prosperity."
[30] Page 68, l. 1413 to p. 69, l. 1456. His source was probably Mandeville's *Voyages*. See text, Appendix II.          [31] Page 68, l. 1429.
[32] Page 69, ll. 1451-52.          [33] Cf. Gierke, *op. cit.*, p. 2.

a kind of exalted being, "aliquod unum quod non est pars," [34] the "divinae maiestatis imago," [35] whose "omnis potestas a Domino Deo est." [36] Just a century before *Mum and the Sothsegger* the theory that kings ruled by divine right was set forth in France by Raoul of Praelles and John of Paris in defense of Philip the Fair against Boniface VIII. In England, Wycliffe was among the first to stress the divine right theory, with his famous doctrine of dominion as founded in grace.[37] And in his interpretation of the theory he added the important doctrine that the king, who is king by virtue of his pre-eminent righteousness, may be said to be above human law, since he is lawmaker for his people.[38] However, since his duty is to decree just laws,[39] made in conformity with God's law,[40] and to set a good example by obeying them,[41] he may also be said to be subject to his own law by virtue of the commands of divine law, though not by those of his own law.[42] But to Wycliffe every righteous man was a lord, so that actually his theory of dominion, establishing a direct relation between man and God, threatened to sweep away both civil rule and priesthood and hence was an ideal only. To most of these earlier theorists the king is the lawmaker, not the people or their representatives. The medieval Church doctrine that the Fall of Man terminated man's state of innocence and equality and thereby instituted lordship strengthened the theory that the people had lost whatever power of government they had at Creation and were subject to the will of the monarch so long as he performed his divinely appointed duties. As representatives of God on earth,

[34] Dante, *De Monarchia*, ed. Moore, p. 344.

[35] John of Salisbury, *Polycraticus*, ed. Webb, I, 235.

[36] *Ibid*. Also Wycliffe, *De Civili Dominio*, ed. Poole, p. 188, and Thomas Aquinas, *De Regimine Principum*, transl. G. B. Phelan, pp. 75, 89.

[37] *De Civili Dominio*, ed. Poole, pp. 125–28. Cf. Carlyle, *op. cit.*, VI, 51–62, and Dunning, *op. cit.*, pp. 260–65.

[38] *De Officio Regis*, ed. Pollard and Sayle, p. 95.

[39] *Ibid.*, p. 96.                    [40] *Ibid*.

[41] *De Civili Dominio*, ed. Poole, p. 188.

[42] *De Officio Regis*, ed. Pollard and Sayle, p. 94. The conflict in later centuries as to the monarch's position under the law was the result of a misunderstanding of Bracton, who did not fail to assert that the king was "sub deo et sub lege quia lex facit regem," *Bracton de Legibus et Consuetudinibus Angliae*, ed. George E. Woodbine (New Haven: Yale University Press, 1915–42), II, 33.

kings were declared to be responsible for the safety and welfare of their subjects, and in return they should receive the love and obedience of their subjects.[43] If the king proved a tyrant, it was thought best to endure him, if possible, lest a worse one appear; but if he became unbearable, the community might proceed against him, not by private means, but by public authority. Such a king, set up by the people, might justly be destroyed by the people or his power be restricted,[44] since the good of the multitude is greater and more divine than the good of one man.[45]

With some of the theories of these earlier writers about monarchy the author of *Mum* is plainly in agreement. Though he has little to say of Richard's or Henry's being God's representative on earth, ruling by divine right or because of pre-eminent goodness, and prefers to rest his defense of monarchy on reason and the practical need for unity, he, too, says that the king's chief duty is to maintain law and order, just as surely as it is the duty of unlearned men to labor at their plows;[46] that in return for his care for the safety and welfare of his subjects the king should receive their love and allegiance;[47] but that if the king should fail in his duty of maintaining law and order and the common welfare, he might be deposed, as Richard had been, and another monarch be chosen, more fit "by kynde," to protect them.[48] The theory of an indefeasible hereditary right to the throne was still not fixed and was not fixed in England until the defeat of the House of Lancaster in the Wars of the Roses established the succession by primogeniture rather than by act of Parliament. Later, in the days of the Stuarts, that theory was to be the first tenet in their theory of divine right.

In several important respects, however, the author of *Mum* is plainly not in accord with these earlier theorists. His monarch is one who rules by a kind of contractual agreement with the people, who is not lawmaker but enforcer of the law made by the representatives

---

[43] Cf. Thomas Aquinas, *De Regimine Principum*, transl. G. B. Phelan, Book I, chaps. x–xiii. On "Thomas Aquinas' Theory of Law and Justice" see Dunning, *op. cit.*, pp. 189–207.     [44] *Ibid.*, pp. 56–60.
[45] *Ibid.*, p. 74.     [46] Page 20, l. 267.
[47] Page 1, ll. 23–26; p. 2, ll. 47–49; p. 4, l. 24; p. 9, ll. 67–68; p. 33, ll. 193–95, etc.
[48] Page 3, l. 1 to p. 4, l. 24; p. 12, ll. 190–92; p. 14, l. 55 to p. 15, l. 85.

of the people, and who is, like the people, subject to the law. In these beliefs he is much more like such democratic theorists as William of Ockham, Marsilius of Padua, and Nicholas of Cusa, who, in their insistence on the rights of the governed, give later medieval political theory its tone of modernity.[49] To all of them, the matter of civil government is a very practical matter, and they speak of it as a natural state that exists, not "dei opere vel oraculo immediate," [50] but "de legum et principatuum institutione tantummodo, quae immediate proveniunt ex arbitrio humanae mentis." [51] The "sententia divini Aristotelis" as stated in his *Politics* is plainly the chief authority of these theorists.[52] The necessity of man-made law in such a state is obvious, according to these theorists, and the people, either all of them or their elected representatives in a general assembly, are the "legislator": "Nos autem dicamus . . . legislatorem seu causam legis effectivam primam et propriam esse populum seu civium universitatem, aut eius valentiorem partem per suam electionem seu voluntatem in generali civium congregatione." [53] Such representation, moreover, should be in "number and quality"—a thing never heard of before.[54] Writing in Paris and no doubt strongly influenced by the political speculation of William of Ockham,[55] who went from Oxford to Paris, Marsilius developed his theories mainly from observing the practices of the Italian City-States; but he is careful to speak of his theories as those "civitatis seu regni." [56] Ockham applied these democratic principles to Church Councils as well as civil assemblies—going so far as to declare that even women should sit as representatives if the need arose.[57] A

---

[49] Cf. Carlyle, *op. cit.*, pp. 7–12, 40–51 and Dunning, *op. cit.*, pp. 238–53. See also Previté-Orton's "Marsilius of Padua," *loc. cit.*, where Marsilius' modernity is stressed as that of "the most radical of the theorists on Church and State in the Middle Ages" (p. 1).

[50] Marsilius of Padua, *Defensor Pacis*, ed. Previté-Orton, p. 48.

[51] *Ibid.*                       [52] *Ibid.*, pp. 15, 40–41, 49, and elsewhere.

[53] *Ibid.*, p. 49.               [54] *Ibid.*, p. 15.

[55] Reginald L. Poole, "William of Ockham," *DNB* (London: Oxford University Press, 1921–22), XIV, 802.

[56] *Defensor Pacis*, ed. Previté-Orton, p. 15.

[57] Gierke, *op. cit.*, p. 59, refers the reader to Ockham's *Dialogus*, I, 6, c. 85, in Goldast's *Monarchia s. Romani Imperii* (Frankfort, 1614), II, 398 ff. The *Dialogus*, however, has not been reprinted and is therefore inaccessible to most readers.

century later, Nicholas of Cusa, a German of wide learning, in a work as revolutionary as Marsilius', strengthened this theory of popular sovereignty by his thesis that the nearer the representative or official is to those he represents, the more nearly he represents them.[58]

The author of *Mum and the Sothsegger,* having seen the deposition of one monarch, who reigned by hereditary right, and the election of another by act of Commons and Lords, seems to have no doubt of the contractual relation between king and people and of the legislative capacity of the representatives of the people in Parliament assembled and of the duty of the king to abide by and enforce all the laws of the realm.[59] However, his purpose is to warn both king and realm that these functions of government are not operating as they should. In the first place, the representatives of the people in Parliament assembled are not truly representing the people, for in Richard's day Parliaments were packed with Richard's yes-men,[60] and in Henry's reign the representatives sent to Parliament for the express purpose of setting forth the people's grievances are silent

---

[58] *De Concordantia Catholica,* ed. Gerhardus Kallen, Books II and III. Though Books II and III are not included in Vol. XIV of the *Opera Omnia* and the plans for printing and distributing those books have no doubt been interrupted by the war, the Registrum of the first three books is included and is remarkable for its indication of the author's democratic ideas. The following chapter headings are especially significant: Book II, chap. viii—"Quod auctoritas in conciliis non dependet a capite concilii, sed communi omnium consensu"; Book II, chap. xiv—"Quod omnis constitutio ex radice naturalis iuris locum habet, et quod omnis coerctio, cum natura aeque liberi simus, ex electione et consensu subiectorum sit"; Book II, chap. xix—"Quod libertas electionis est radix, per quam omnis ordinata potestas constituitur"; and Book III, chap. xii—"Quod rex aut princeps leges et statuta generalia provinciam respicientia in generalibus utriusque status sui regni conciliis per consensum edere habet et illa salva epikeia exequi et defensare, et quod cotidianum concilium de electis ex tota provincia subiecta de consensu universalis sui concilii habere debeat."

[59] A good idea of the degree of democracy achieved in representation in Parliament in the fifteenth century may be secured from the *History of Parliament. Biographies of the Members of the Commons House 1439–1509* (London: H. M. Stationery Office, 1936), Vol. I, Intro. by Josiah C. Wedgwood. Since elections were mainly by acclamation and there was "no scrutiny of a man's right to shout" (p. xlvii); since every kind of trade except soap boilers had members sitting in Parliament (p. xxxvi); and since Parliament was a place where Ministers and people mingled informally on equal terms, while they told each other their grievances (p. v), it would seem that representation had a pretty important place in the government—unless it was interfered with by bribery.                                                      [60] Page 24, l. 20 to p. 26, l. 93.

for fear of what may happen to them.[61] Secondly, the king is not enforcing the laws. And finally, as a result of the king's failure to enforce the laws, the courts of law are full of bribery and deceit.[62] The failure of Parliament to provide the necessary statutes for reform, the failure of the king to enforce the laws, and the failure of the courts to proceed honestly and justly—all these conditions destroy respect for law and government and so threaten the monarchy itself. Of what use are laws without enforcement? [63] And surely the greatest boon on earth is just laws concerning the management of revenues.[64] If Richard and Henry had only maintained the court revenues according to law, they would not have had to demand subsidies from Parliament or collect taxes without Parliament's authorization, such as those on imports and exports and personal property and the cloth at the fairs, or demand in time of peace the old feudal taxes on towns provided for time of war, or demand forced loans, or send tax collectors armed with poleaxes to collect taxes from their laborers by threats and violence and thus make the people hate the tax collectors.

In this connection it should be pointed out that the sympathy of the author of *Mum* throughout his advice on good government is with the poor. Though *Mum and the Sothsegger* seems in one instance unsympathetic,[65] the contrary is true. In that one instance, near the close of the second fragment,[66] the author chides those of the commons who ignorantly criticize the king's government and make false statements about it as indulging in conduct against Natural Law; [67] but he hastens to add that he is not speaking of their representatives, whose duty it is, in Parliament and in the king's Council, to set forth the wrongs of the realm.[68] In the very place provided for such discussion, the representatives of the people are silent. Nevertheless, the poor who spread lies about the king

---

[61] Page 60, ll. 1129–40. *The History of Parliament, loc. cit.,* Intro., p. v, provides vivid corroboration of this charge.

[62] Page 60, ll. 1141–48; p. 70, l. 1489 to p. 77, l. 1722.

[63] Page 75, ll. 1646–47.      [64] Page 19, ll. 241–42.

[65] See eds.' Intro., p. xvi.      [66] Page 67, ll. 1389–1488.

[67] Page 69, ll. 1457–59.      [68] Page 69, l. 1460.

and lords gain nothing but resentment, and in the end they stir
up mean thoughts among the rest of the commons and even turn
the lords from their duty of defending the realm. Thus all suffer,
commons as well as lords. To offset this one charge that the author
of *Mum* makes against *some* of the commons, he repeatedly urges
the cause of "the poor." It is they who suffer most from poor government. The lords and the clergy have taken care of themselves very
well, but the poor commons are everywhere set upon and deserve
the king's protection first and foremost. In at least thirty instances
the author speaks of the plundering of the poor by the king's tax
collectors, by the king's judges and justices, by lawyers, by the
clergy, by town officials, by the lesser gentry, and by the lords.
Moreover, the poor have a multitude of truthtellers who are constantly telling them their faults, whereas their superiors have none.
If the author of *Mum* charges some of the commons with harmful
gossiping, it is in a spirit of concern for the welfare of all estates,
including the commons, that he does so, rather than with "contempt."[69] May "harde happes" fall on those who so injure Henry
or any lord of the land "that loueth pees and reste,"[70] he says, and
the last phrase is significant, for not all the lords did so love peace
and rest. At the same time, he praises the truthteller, of whatever
rank he may be, provided only that he know the truth and tell it
for the good of the king and his people: "But yif God haue grauntyd
the / grace for to knowe Ony manere mysscheff / that myghtte be
amendyd, Schewe that to thi souereyne / to schelde him from
harmes."[71] By such truthtellers the people should be represented
in Parliament and Council and in courts of law, so that they would
have no need to grumble and falsify and thus destroy the necessary
loyalty among all estates. As in *Piers Plowman,* the commons in *Mum*
also have a very definite and important part in the government,
and as a legist rather than a religious allegorist the author of *Mum*
makes clear that the real power of the people lies in their representation in Parliament and not in malicious gossip and disloyalty.

[69] Eds.' Intro., p. xvi.     [70] Page 67, l. 1405 to p. 68, l. 1406.
[71] Page 9, ll. 72–75.

In all his discussion of the duties of the king as ruler of his people, the author of *Mum* never forgets to stress similarly the duties of the people to their king. Strangely enough, though it was against feudalism, with its troublesome division of power, that the author of *Mum* chiefly contended, it was to the nature of the feudal relation that the theory of contract between monarch and people partly owed its acceptance and development.[72] Even the author of *Mum* speaks of the relation between people and monarch in terms that savor of feudalism. Instead of several lords, however, the realm now has one. To him all owe allegiance—nobles, clergy, and commons. The author himself is well aware of his own duty of allegiance. For example, he pitied Richard until Christ required it no longer,[73] and as a liege to his lord, he served Richard loyally while he reigned.[74] Not only his body and his beasts belong to his king, but also his good counsel.[75] To Henry, too, he owes allegiance and counsel.[76] All the people, likewise, owe allegiance and love. Allegiance without love avails little.[77] Thus the feudal doctrine of love between estates is applied to the relation of people to monarch.

The author's doctrine of popular sovereignty and the contractual relation between people and monarch, like his doctrine of the necessity of a single Head, is enforced by: (1) his references to the Body Politic and the effect each member has on all the rest; (2) the gardener's account of the good government of the bee "king," who rules through agreement of the company that unites all in one; and (3) the example of Jhengiz Khan, who called a council of representatives and worked with them as wise men should, to restore the realm.

Since, to the author of *Mum,* a monarchy limited by such contractual relationship between king and people is the only true monarchy, and since the contractual relationship can be maintained only by due process of law, it is in this matter of the law that the author of *Mum* makes some of his most serious charges and offers his most helpful advice to the king. Next to the inroads of feudal barons on the

---

[72] Cf. Figgis, *op. cit.,* p. 31; also Fritz Kern, *Kingship and Law in the Middle Ages,* transl. S. B. Chrimes (Oxford: B. Blackwell, 1939), pp. 121–22; also Carlyle, *op. cit.,* II, 74.     [73] Page 1, ll. 23–24.     [74] Page 1, ll. 25–26.
[75] Page 2, ll. 47–49.     [76] Page 33, ll. 193–95.     [77] Page 4, l. 24.

king's authority, this is the problem that looms largest in his mind. Richard led his own life lawlessly,[78] and it is best for Henry, king by Parliamentary title, to remember that the people will "loue you for the lawe,"[79] lest marvels befall him, too—probably deposition—within a few years.[80]

Nor is the author of *Mum* concerned only with English case law in his denunciations of lawless rule. Like all medieval political theorists, he makes the distinction between man-made or Positive Law and God-made or Natural Law.[81] The idea of Natural Law, sometimes also called the *Ius Divinum* from the theologian's point of view or the *Ius Commune Gentium* from the point of view of the classicist, is a matter somewhat difficult for modern readers to understand, but it is essential to interpretation of medieval literature of political import. To the modern reader, familiar with one kind of law, derived from legislative statutes and court decisions, another legal standard, above such man-made law, more exalted and more binding, is something of an anomaly. Nevertheless, in the Middle Ages, Natural Law was the most valid law. It was recognized by courts and justices and was binding on all, sovereign and subject alike. Since God, not the State, was the source of all law, Natural Law was thought of as part of the world order from the beginning and as unchangeable. This Natural Law was therefore very old law and also good law, and when a case arose in court which no man-made law would cover, a new law was made with the idea that the new law was simply man's expression of the good old law, implicit in life itself. Thus lawmakers, both courts and legislative bodies alike, did not create law, but discovered the old and gave it clarity and force by putting it into the form of Positive Law.[82]

[78] Page 3, ll. 12–13.    [79] Page 27, l. 26.    [80] Page 34, ll. 221–22.

[81] Cf. Gierke, *Political Theories of the Middle Age*, p. 73; also Otto von Gierke, *The Development of Political Theory*, transl. Bernard Freyd (New York: W. W. Norton & Co., 1939), pp. 299–307.

[82] For an excellent brief review of the history of the conception of Natural Law see Otto von Gierke's *Natural Law and the Theory of Society 1500 to 1800*, transl. with Intro. by Ernest Barker (Cambridge [Eng.]: University Press, 1934), Intro., pp. xxxiv–xlvi. Cf. also Fritz Kern, *Kingship and Law in the Middle Ages*, ed. S. B. Chrimes, pp. 149–80; James Bryce, *Studies in History and Jurisprudence* (London and New York: Oxford University Press, 1901), pp. 562–97; A. J. Carlyle, *Political Liberty, a*

Protected by Natural Law, any subject might theoretically question
in court an act of government that to him seemed unlawful or
unjust and obtain redress on the basis of what he considered his
just rights, whether petty or important.[83] Today a plaintiff's idea
of what is just or unjust law has little weight unless he can secure
revision of the Positive Law by some legislative body. By the modern
reader, the medieval conception of Natural Law would probably
be described as the "right" or the "ethical" or the "honest" thing to
do, but not as necessarily the legal thing to do. Nevertheless, the
medieval idea of the importance of Natural Law to Positive Law
has never been lost, and earnest pleas for the constant reincorporation
of that law in modern man-made law are familiar to modern legists.[84]

The problem of the medieval legist was still further complicated
by the distinction between Roman law, the *Corpus Juris Civilis* of
Justinian, and the ancient customary law of such countries as were
not subjugated by Rome. Although in England, as we have seen,
English common law was preserved when Roman law threatened
to replace it, in the twelfth century and later, most of the countries
of Europe, including Scotland, adopted or "received" Roman civil
law, and it became the legal standard for a large part of Europe.
Legists in other countries as well, including England, fascinated
by the reasonableness and clarity of Roman law, assumed that it
might be and should be used as supplementary to the law of national

---

*History of the Conception in the Middle Ages and Modern Times* (Oxford: Clarendon
Press, 1941), pp. 12–16; Max Shepard, "William of Occam and the Higher Law,"
*American Political Science Review*, XXVI, No. 6 (1932), 1005–23.

[83] Cf. *Mum and the Sothsegger*, p. 74, ll. 1617–18.

[84] For an interesting discussion of the "Law of Nature in the Modern World" see
Scott, *op. cit.*, I, 264–70, and Bryce, *op. cit.*, pp. 597–606. See also the plea of Otto
von Gierke for the necessary union of Natural and Positive Law in *Natural Law and
the Theory of Society*, Appendix II, pp. 223–26. The beneficial effects of the concept
of Natural Law in medieval political theory are discussed by Ewart Lewis, "Natural
Law and Expediency in Medieval Political Theory," *Ethics*, I, No. 2 (1940), 144–63:
"But, whatever the extent of its influence, the appeal to natural law certainly helped to
break the sway of irrational custom and tradition over the medieval mind and to
substitute the sovereignty of reason and utility. . . . And if such a natural law is to
have any usefulness as 'a sort of rule or measure' in our swiftly moving world, I suggest
that it might well follow the pattern of natural law in medieval theory: affirming in-
violable ends for mankind but allowing the utmost flexibility in the choice of means"
(pp. 162–63).

custom. Especially did they urge such use because a large part of Roman law, and the most useful part, seemed to claim to be the law of no one nation, but of all nations and all men, a kind of Law of Nature, and so, to Christians, a Law of God.[85] Nor were the Italian legists slow to urge its universality. Thus the medieval conception of Natural Law, derived from the Greeks[86] and most thoroughly defined by Thomas Aquinas,[87] was gradually supplemented and strengthened by the legists' knowledge of Roman law or the *Ius Civile;* and what to the modern reader may seem to have been merely ethical theory became more and more fixed as a legal standard.

When it is recalled that the *Corpus Juris Canonici,* compiled in 1140 by Gratian, the Benedictine monk of Bologna, for use in the University of Bologna, governed such civil matters as marriage and divorce and the probating of wills, it is easy to see that the problem of the medieval jurist was even further complicated. He should know the law of the Church as well, especially in so far as it related to civil rights and duties. Violations of Canon Law concerning civil matters might even be tried in civil courts, but the law itself was the will of the Church, and hence other distinctions crept in that further complicated enforcement.

Against such a background of legal distinctions the author of *Mum* shows his king how the law has been violated and what must be done to provide justice and sound government. Concerning the dignity and authority of the law itself he has little doubt; his charge is the lack of enforcement by courts and king alike. When he complains of some wrongs done, he does so to suggest the need of new laws to cover such cases. In one instance only, I believe, does he criticize the law itself. On that occasion he finds fault with the English law that permits a man to bring suit whenever he sees fit. As a result, the courts are burdened with unnecessary and foolish

---

[85] "Ius naturale est quod natura, id est ipse deus docuit omnia naturalia," says Henry de Bracton, *Bracton de Legibus et Consuetudinibus Angliae,* ed. Woodbine, II, 26.

[86] Gierke, *Natural Law and the Theory of Society,* Intro., pp. xxxiv–xxxvi.

[87] *Opera Omnia* (Rome: Ex Typographia Polyglotta S. C. de Propaganda Fide, 1882–1930), VII, 149–222.

cases. Civil law, he says, does not approve; and by Civil Law, as
we have seen, he means Roman law, which has come to be considered
as Natural Law or the *Ius Commune Gentium:*

> But ciuile seith vs not so / that serueth for al peuple
> That habiteth vndre heuene / hethen men and other.[88]

And Canon Law and the Gospel are against it:

> And Crist-is lawe-is y-canonized canon, yf thou loke,
> And eeke the glorious gospelle / grovnde of all lawes.[89]

Consequently, he says, he has never been able to persuade himself
that the English law is not out of line in this respect:

> For in my conscience ne in my credo yit couthe I neuer vele
> But that oure lawe leneth there a lite, as me thenketh.[90]

He knows, too, how the law can be made a subterfuge, to cover
and color the tricks of these habitual litigants,[91] but such malpractice
is the fault of the court and not of the law itself.

In speaking of the requirements of Natural Law, the author
usually labels them as being "according to nature" or "against nature"
or a "natural cause." For example, unless the crown "in his kinde" [92]
have his revenues restored to him, no one will prosper. And when
the author condemns the outrages committed by Richard's evil
councillors against the wise courtiers of the realm, he recites what
is evidently a law to him, namely, that the greatest misdeed on earth
is that done "aȝeins kynde." [93] Similarly he says that there is no
"kindely cause" [94] why the commons should oppose or criticize the
king. Bolingbroke, the Eagle, has been chosen as king because he
was "heed of hem all / and hieste of kynde," [95] just as the bees
also chose their king "by kinde." [96] In addition to such direct references to the law of "kinde," the author cites the dictates of Natural

[88] Page 74, ll. 1619–20.     [89] Page 74, ll. 1621–22.     [90] Page 74, ll. 1624–25.
[91] Page 73, l. 1592.     [92] Page 75, l. 1675.     [93] Page 13, l. 10.
[94] Page 69, l. 1458. "Cause" is used like the Latin legal *causa,* meaning "case."
[95] Page 15, l. 92.     [96] Page 56, l. 999.

Law as those of "reason"[97] and "wisdom" and "pure necessity." Reason says: that it is best to have one ruler;[98] that it is not for a subject to annoy his king in deed or word,[99] though he may offer good counsel if he has it;[100] and that each estate should perform its own work in the realm.[101] A third method of indicating the dictates of Natural Law is that of speaking of the "duties" of king and subjects, or of what they "should" do if they are to do what is right. In this sense, the author falls into the parlance of other literature of estates and of the doctrines of feudal society. When he says that "who so loketh on the lawe may lerne, yf hym like, Thayre ordre and office / and how thay [ought] wyrche,"[102] it is of the law of natural duty that he speaks, rather than of any court decision or legislative action, and hence in the next few lines it is in a chronicle of clerks' and kings' lines that he finds his evidence for belief that clergy and knighthood especially are no longer what they were in the days of their forefathers. The duty of the king, to study law and keep order, the duty of the lords to defend the realm, the duty of the clergy to serve as spiritual "lanterns"[103] for men to live by, and the duty of the commons to labor for the rest are all cited as matters of common understanding, as "Crist dide thaym stable,"[104] rather than anything that needs to be proved or disproved in a court of law.

Nevertheless, as a result of such common understanding of the requirements of Natural Law, which no one, whether king or subjects, may escape, some definite laws have been devised, by human agencies, and so the author has much to say about Positive Law, as it is administered or violated in the courts. His references to Positive Law, or the laws established by court precedent and legislation, concern three main subjects: taxation, the administration of justice, and representation in Parliament. Richard and his councillors violated the laws of all those three phases of government by

[97] Cf. Scott, op. cit., I, 269: "The law natural has long been tacitly or indirectly recognized in English jurisprudence—though usually under the alias of 'right reason' or 'the law of reason.'"    [98] Page 74, l. 1629.    [99] Page 9, ll. 68–69.
[100] Page 2, l. 48.    [101] Page 20, l. 254.    [102] Page 77, l. 1740–41.
[103] Page 78, l. 1749.    [104] Page 77, l. 1739.

forcibly collecting unauthorized taxes, by disrupting court procedure, and by calling packed Parliaments where the forms were all adhered to for the sake of appearance, but where representatives were not duly chosen and so spoke only as they were told. In Henry's reign the disorders continue, and the laws go unenforced. Especially do the injustices of court practice and the loss of the king's revenues concern the author of *Mum* in Henry's reign.

> Not-wi[th]standing statutz full strattely y-made
> To stable many statutz and strong lawes make,[105]

Henry's greedy councillors and also the bishops, the "lordz y-lettred of oone lawe and other,"[106] that is, in both Canon and Civil Law, rob him of his revenues. As a result, the commons are still plundered, and the king must live on his laborers, a thing that "may not long indure."[107]

Whereas in Richard's reign brawlers wearing the king's badge upset all court procedure and administered the law with swords and clubs, the courts in Henry's reign administer justice according to the bribes they receive.[108] The poor, lacking such fees, lose all the suits they bring. The lords bribe the lawyers to deceive men and break agreements made by friendly settlement. The lords, by threat of loss of pay and employment, force their squires to testify for them, no matter where justice or the truth lies. People are bribed to shove and create disorder at the assizes so that the poor householder who is being sued loses his very house. It is better for a poor man, sued by his superior, to lose the suit than to be sued repeatedly and finally lose everything. Lords contend against each other endlessly to save their hurt pride, though they would win more respect if it were known that they refused to go to law without good cause. Such legal disorders could be ended if everyone bringing suit needlessly were fined and if the costs of the suit must be paid as soon as the case ended. The king's failure to enforce the law can have only one result: the loss of the allegiance of the people; and the

[105] Page 74, ll. 1641–42.
[106] Page 75, l. 1649.
[107] Page 75, l. 1668.
[108] Page 70, l. 1489 to p. 74, l. 1625.

loss of the allegiance of the people may mean the end of monarchy; for how can the king himself contend with the "great ones" if the people have deserted him?

Meanwhile the monarchy is weakened also by the violations, by both priests and prelates, of the Canon Law. They violate the law of tithes by keeping all of them for themselves. Though "lewed and lettrid ful lite," [109] the author of *Mum* himself can cite the law about tithes in only three lines and not a letter more: Give God's third to God's people, the poor; keep one third for your own sustenance; and use one third for the upkeep of the Church.[110] Surely the clergy should be able to remember so short a law. The bishops violate the Canon Law by buying and selling benefices.[111] They live luxuriously and spend on mistresses what should go to the poor and the sick."[112] They take bribes for permitting other men to have mistresses, and then have to lie about it, "for lawe was hit neuer."[113] The Archdeacon, for bribes, condones the errors and immorality of his priests and parsons, who thus so weaken the authority of Canon Law that ignorant men, following their example, break the Ten Commandments. Of the violations of Canon Law concerning the probating of wills the author of *Mum* is also informed. When the will has been validated by the seal of the bishop's registry and all the fees paid, the clerks toss it into a chest lest it be copied and executed. Though the will may bequeath a fifteenth of the estate to charity, one receipt only is given, and the executors never execute the will, but keep all the property for themselves. The appearance of Mum to the author in bishop's mitre raises the question of whether the author of *Mum* himself may not have been warned by the clergy for his attacks on such violations of Canon Law.[114]

What is perhaps most significant about *Mum and the Sothsegger* is that, in the midst of such far-reaching constitutional changes as

---

[109] Page 46, l. 652.    [110] Page 46, ll. 657–60.    [111] Page 66, l. 1372.
[112] Page 67, ll. 1379–80.    [113] Page 66, l. 1352.
[114] However, he cites the testimony of one bishop, Richard Fitzralph, Archbishop of Armagh, in his attack on the friars. Fitzralph, best known as the center of feeling against the friars in the fourteenth century, was also probably the source of Wycliffe's theory of Dominion. Wycliffe revered him as a teacher and often spoke of him with respect and admiration.

were achieved in the late fourteenth and early fifteenth centuries in England, it was possible for this poet-legist to think and write about law and make distinctions and suggest practical changes and, above all, to sense the importance to monarchy, if it was to survive, of a lawful rule through recognition of the powers of Parliament. In so far as he was able, like Marsilius of Padua and William of Ockham, to sense the dangers of monarchy absolute and unchecked by the will of the people and to set forth the advantages of a monarchy so limited, as the prematurely constitutional reign of Henry IV promised to provide them, the author of *Mum* was liberal and forward-looking. Indeed he says of his book of government that he writes "Of maters that I thenke / to meve for the best For kyngis and kayseris / comynge here-after."[115] On the other hand, in an age when Lollard zeal for reform brought renewed hangings and burnings, the author of *Mum* seems calmly conservative. Nevertheless, his theories of monarchy were those of the medieval theorists who looked forward to the modern democratic state rather than backward to the days of feudal and monarchical tyranny.

[115]Page 6, ll. 84–85

# THE THEME OF "PARADISE LOST"

THE FACT that the theme or central meaning of *Paradise Lost* has been and still is far less generally understood than we may suppose has been indicated by scholars and critics alike.[1] Professor E. M. W. Tillyard, in 1930, without stating his own choice of theme, noted that critics of earlier generations have concerned themselves with almost every other phase of the epic except its central meaning, assuming perhaps that "the meaning appeared too simple to need discussion," [2] since Milton himself seems to tell us all we need to know about it in his opening lines. In 1941 Logan Pearsall Smith's little volume on *Milton and His Modern Critics* raised the hopes of many that some day the peculiar, often ridiculous assumptions of such modern critics of Milton as Ezra Pound, T. S. Eliot, Middleton Murry, Herbert Read, and Frank Leavis would be adequately answered. In a warning against superficial assumptions of all kinds Professor A. S. P. Woodhouse, in 1944, discussed the true bases for expository criticism and said that it is "fatal to assume that Milton is merely rehearsing and embellishing the Hebrew-Christian myth of the fall or that *Paradise Lost* is, in Raleigh's phrase, 'a monument to dead ideas.' " [3] In 1944, also, Professor Douglas Bush, in the Messenger Lectures on the Evolution of Civilization, at Cornell,[4] warned against the "ex-cathedra utterances" of such critics as T. S. Eliot and Lord David Cecil, against the mistaken nineteenth-

---

[1] Cf., among others, E. M. W. Tillyard, *Milton* (London: Chatto and Windus, 1930), pp. 237 ff.; A. S. P. Woodhouse, "The Approach to Milton," *Transactions of the Royal Society of Canada*, XXXVIII (May, 1944), sec. 2, 201–13; Logan Pearsall Smith, *Milton and His Modern Critics* (Boston: Little, Brown and Company, 1941), pp. 45 ff.; Douglas Bush, *Paradise Lost in Our Time* (Ithaca: Cornell University Press, 1945), chap. i; Douglas Bush, *English Literature in the Earlier Seventeenth Century, 1600–1660* (Oxford: Clarendon Press, 1945), pp. 379 ff.; A. J. A. Waldock, *Paradise Lost and Its Critics* (Cambridge [Eng.]: University Press, 1947), pp. 1–24.

[2] Tillyard, *op. cit.*, p. 237.     [3] "The Approach to Milton," *loc. cit.*, p. 206.

[4] Published under the title of *Paradise Lost in Our Time*.

century notion still prevalent among most general readers here as
well as in England of "verbal and musical beauties divorced from
obsolete substance," and against the "monotonous glibness" with
which "a good many bright American undergraduates pour forth
the 'metaphysical' and anti-Miltonist creed." [5] In 1945, in his discussion of *English Literature in the Earlier Seventeenth Century,*
Professor Bush again pointed out, in more detail, some of the absurd
ideas concerning the meaning of *Paradise Lost* as a preliminary to
his own interpretation.[6] Professor Bush's own statement of "Milton's
whole theme" as that of "pride and presumption" seems, however,
too narrow and too negative to satisfy most readers. It is part of
the story, but not all of it, as the rest of Professor Bush's interpretation clearly implies. In 1946 Mark Van Doren's *The Noble
Voice* [7] and in 1947 A. J. A. Waldock's *Paradise Lost and Its Critics* [8]
both showed such uncertainty as to the real theme of *Paradise Lost*
as to cause both to conclude that Milton himself did not know
what he meant and that, therefore, the poem is full of inconsistencies
and other deficiencies. Assuming that Milton's theme is original
sin, Professor Van Doren concluded that Milton is "only half sure
of what he understands and sees" and hence limps along lamely
at the end of the procession of the nine "noble voices" discussed.
One wonders finally how Milton, not a "maker" but a mere "ma-
gician," got into the volume at all. Professor Waldock, closely
paralleling Professor Van Doren's argument, concludes that the
*Paradise Lost* that Milton meant is not the *Paradise Lost* that Milton
wrote, because "the *Paradise Lost* that he meant was, in a strict sense,
unwritable." Here is confusion twice confounded!

Some of the results of this prevailing uncertainty as to what
*Paradise Lost* really says or as to what Milton's purpose was in
writing the poem are: (1) a wide diversity of opinion among critics
and scholars as to its theme, (2) frequent misunderstanding and
disparagement of it as a work of art, and (3) difficulty among

[5] *Ibid.,* p. 25.                   [6] Pages 379 ff.
[7] New York: Henry Holt and Company, 1946, pp. 122–47.
[8] Pages 1–24.

readers generally in understanding the poem and among teachers and students in the classroom particularly, in interpreting the poem in a satisfactory or impressive manner. The purpose and central idea of any work determine in large measure its interest and significance for us, and a wrong interpretation of its theme may prevent its being read. The reader, finding such diverse statements concerning *Paradise Lost* as that it is simply the story of the Hebrew-Christian myth of the fall of man,[9] or that it is a sermon on temperance,[10] or that it concerns the conflict of reason and passion in man,[11] or that its theme is not Paradise Lost, but Paradise,[12] or that it is a pamphlet on many subjects, by an author whose "tremendous imagination penetrates chaos and the spheres, but never the human soul," [13] or that its "explicit theme is a cosmic disharmony," [14] or that the poem is "an artistic failure," [15] or that today we read *Paradise Lost* only for its craftsmanship and style,[16] or that Milton fails when he tries to justify the ways of God to man and would have been more successful if he had tried to justify the ways of man to God [17]—in the face of such diversity of interpretation, the reader is not likely to read the poem at all. And the teacher who attempts to present the epic with no more understanding than some of the above statements indicate will surely leave no true or significant or enduring impression of its worth. In view of the numerous present-day misconceptions concerning *Paradise Lost,* it seems highly important that its theme and purpose be as clearly conceived

---

[9] H. W. Peck, "The Theme of *Paradise Lost,*" *PMLA,* N.S., XXII (1914), 256–69.

[10] E. A. Greenlaw, "A Better Teacher than Aquinas," *Studies in Philology,* XIV (April, 1917), 215.

[11] H. J. C. Grierson, *Cross Currents in English Literature of the Seventeenth Century* (London: Chatto and Windus, 1929), p. 231.

[12] Paul Elmer More, "The Theme of *Paradise Lost,*" *Shelburne Essays,* 4th series (New York: G. P. Putnam's Sons, 1907), pp. 239–53.

[13] Rose Macaulay, *Milton* (London: Duckworth, 1934), p. 140.

[14] G. Wilson Knight, *The Burning Oracle* (London: Oxford University Press, 1939), chap. iii, "The Frozen Labyrinth: an Essay on Milton," pp. 59–113.

[15] Mark Van Doren in an address before the National Council of Teachers of English.

[16] T. S. Eliot, *After Strange Gods* (London: Faber and Faber, 1934), p. 35.

[17] Allen Tate on an "Invitation to Learning" radio program, *Invitation to Learning* (New York: Randon House, 1941), pp. 307–21.

and stated as possible. The greater the length of a work and the profounder its theme, the more difficult the problem becomes. Nevertheless, the ability to conceive and state clearly its central idea is a first requirement, it seems to me, for complete understanding and appreciation.

The only sure means to a true understanding and appreciation of the epic is, of course, as both Professor E. E. Stoll [18] and Professor Woodhouse [19] have pointed out, historical study. After prolonged investigation and deliberation and after years of teaching Milton and of trying to determine the significance of *Paradise Lost* for students as well as for myself, I have come to the conclusion that Milton's purpose in writing *Paradise Lost* was, briefly, to present the theme of "the making of the greater man" [20]—not simply the greater Man, Christ, as the fourth line of the epic might seem to

---

[18] E. E. Stoll, "Certain Fallacies and Irrelevancies in the Literary Scholarship of the Day," *Poets and Playwrights* (Minneapolis: University of Minnesota Press, 1930), p. 232.

[19] "The Approach to Milton," *loc. cit.,* pp. 203 ff.

[20] I had arrived at this conclusion and had made the first draft of this paper over a year before I saw Professor Bush's *Paradise Lost in Our Time.* It was most interesting, therefore, to find near the end of his first lecture (p. 27) the following statement: "Nowadays old and young are full of zeal for a better world, and that of course is fine. But, to judge from the millions of words poured into print and into the air, much of that zeal is directed toward making other people better, or making more and better gadgets. In all his major poems Milton is occupied with the far more real and fundamental problem of making one's self better. And he makes us better not merely through his imaginative and 'poetical' beauties but through the total effect of his religious and ethical theme, through his profound concern with 'man, the heart of man, and human life.' " Professor Bush does not specifically say that the theme of *Paradise Lost* is "the making of the greater man," but surely his interpretation of Milton's purpose is the same. Later Professor Bush does say (p. 49) that in *Paradise Lost* "Pride and presumption are Milton's whole theme" and (p. 52) that "the theme of *Paradise Lost* is the conflict between pride and religious humility." Here I think the statement of theme is unduly limited; the earlier statement of Milton's general purpose is a clearer one. Though pride may be the theme of the temptation, it is too limited and negative a theme, I believe, for the whole epic. When, in his study of *English Literature in the Earlier Seventeenth Century, 1600-1660,* Professor Bush again says (p. 377) that "Irreligious pride and religious humility are indeed the one great theme of his major poems," he again explicitly limits his statement of theme, though his interpretation elsewhere suggests "the making of the greater man" as in the following (p. 380): "We follow with dramatic fullness the process by which the regal pair (Adam and Eve), created perfect, become Everyman and Everywoman, and we see them on the way to regeneration."

imply, and not the chosen few, predestined to be saved, but the better human being everywhere. There are many reasons why that purpose is understandable and acceptable. Not the least of them is that it is inclusive enough to give the epic unity and hence helps to make it an artistic success. It also provides a place in the epic for the so-called "digressions" and "unnecessary ostentation of learning," to which Addison and others have objected. Moreover, it is a theme having positive force, not indicated even by the title *Paradise Lost*. Instead of being merely a narrative of conflict and loss, it is an epic of spiritual conflict gloriously won. Instead of stressing man's faults and weakness, it is, like Christianity itself, full of faith and hope for the future of humankind. Most important of all, however, is the fact that such a theme makes the epic significant "not of an age, but for all time." If that theme was timely in Milton's day, when greater men were needed so desperately, surely in our day, when it is a truism that mankind has not kept pace socially and spiritually with his achievements in science, the making of "greater men" should be of first importance. In an age when wise leaders are needed throughout the world and when the worth and dignity of the individual and the demand for governments that will respect that dignity are everywhere being asserted, *Paradise Lost* should be recognized as a monument to the most vital ideas of all time—ideas so vital that they cannot safely be ignored.

Before proceeding to an examination of the precise meaning of the phrase "the making of the greater man" and to the evidence for saying that that is Milton's theme in *Paradise Lost,* it will be interesting and helpful to review briefly some of the earlier statements of theme or central meaning. In the light of those statements, most of which assign too narrow a scope to the epic or define a part of the epic instead of the whole, while others are too negative or too pessimistic for so victorious a poem, the true meaning of the epic can be more clearly seen. Some of the earlier statements are, of course, so mistaken as to need little attention, but they, too, belong in such a survey if only to show of what aberrations some critics and scholars have been capable.

In the eighteenth century Pope, Addison, and Johnson, having more to say about *Paradise Lost* as poetry than about its central meaning, analyzed mainly its epic qualities and its versification. As might be expected in a so-called "Age of Enlightenment," the direct outgrowth of the new spirit of scientific self-sufficiency of the latter half of the seventeenth century, most eighteenth-century readers had little understanding of or sympathy for the Puritan doctrine of regeneration that Milton found important for all mankind everywhere and in all ages. However, in his famous *Spectator* papers Addison, pausing at the fourth word of the epic, concluded that its theme is "that obedience to the will of God makes men happy, and that disobedience makes them miserable." As a result of that definition, Addison made Adam and Eve the joint hero of the poem, but he found the conclusion of the narrative unhappy and therefore not suited to a heroic poem, and he criticized the epic for having too many digressions and for "unnecessary ostentation of learning." Dr. Johnson, like Pope and Addison, regarded Milton's opening lines as a simple and easily comprehensible statement of the purpose or central meaning of the epic. "His purpose," says Johnson,[21] "was the most useful and most arduous: *to vindicate the ways of God to man;* to show the reasonableness of religion, and the necessity of obedience to the Divine Law." For Milton's choice of such a purpose and of the Fall of Man as the "fable" by means of which he was to convey this theme, Johnson has only the highest praise. In his admiration for Milton's moral theme, Dr. Johnson grows eloquent, and one feels that he comes closer to a real understanding of *Paradise Lost* than his nineteenth-century successors:

His subject is the fate of worlds, the revolutions of heaven and of earth; rebellion against the Supreme King, raised by the highest

[21] *Lives of the Poets* (London: Oxford University Press, 1938), I, 122.

order of created beings; the overthrow of their host and the punishment of their crime; the creation of a new race of reasonable creatures; their original happiness and innocence, their forfeiture of immortality, and their restoration to hope and peace.

Plainly Dr. Johnson, unlike Addison, did not find the conclusion of *Paradise Lost* unhappy. Neither did he discover digressions or ostentation of learning; he praised *Paradise Lost* as "a full display of the united force of study and genius . . . a book of universal knowledge." [22] In comparing Milton's "sanctity of thought" with the lack of it in the ancient epic poets, who lacked "the light of Revelation," as well as with Ariosto and other Italian writers, who show that "the advantages of even Christian knowledge may be possessed in vain," Dr. Johnson asserts Milton's superiority in teaching justice and mercy rather than the fortitude and prudence of the ancients, and one is impressed by Johnson's insight and appreciation. When he proceeds to enumerate the "defects and faults" of *Paradise Lost,* however, one realizes that all his eloquent praise is only the approval of the rather bored orthodox churchman, to whom "these truths are too important to be new; they have been taught to our infancy. . . . Being therefore not new, they raise no unaccustomed emotion in the mind." [23] In other words, to Dr. Johnson *Paradise Lost* was little more than a paraphrase of Old Testament theology and history, which he no doubt accepted as literal and even uninteresting truth.

The Romanticists and Victorians, dreaming like Milton of better days, regarded the theme of the poem as the conflict of liberty against authority. To them the narrative was no longer significant as theology or history, and hence Milton's doctrines of pride, remorse, faith, and obedience had little meaning. To them Satan was heroic and God was tyrannical, and as a result most of them missed the theme of *Paradise Lost* entirely. Coleridge, like Dr. Johnson, says that "The Fall of Man is the subject; Satan is the cause," and that Milton's object was "to justify the ways of God to man." [24] In his

---

[22] *Ibid.,* p. 131.  [23] *Ibid.,* p. 130.

[24] *Lectures and Notes on Shakespeare and Other English Poets,* ed. T. Ashe (London: George Bell and Sons, 1884), Appendix IV, "Notes on Milton," p. 522.

praise of Milton's "purity of mind and piety absolute," his "keen
love of truth," his "keen love of his country," his "love of man as
a probationer of immortality," in his appreciation of the superiority
of Milton's theme to that of ancient epic and of the fact that the
combat of evil and good in *Paradise Lost* "is wider than Christen-
dom, and comprehends the Jewish and Mohammedan worlds" as
well, Coleridge reveals none of Dr. Johnson's boredom; and he
defends Milton against Pope, remarking that "Pope was hardly
the man to criticize Milton." [25] However, he does imply, in all
his comments, that Milton was the product of an age that was past
and that *Paradise Lost,* in the new age, was somewhat out of date.
"These were, these alone could be, the conditions under which such
a work as the 'Paradise Lost' could be conceived and accomplished,"
he says; and again: "The controversial spirit observable in many
parts of the poem, especially in God's speeches, is immediately
attributable to the great controversy of that age, the origination of
evil." To Coleridge, as to the other Romanticists, Satan had "a
singularity of daring," a "grandeur of sufferance, and a ruined
splendour, which constitute the very height of poetic sublimity." [26]
Hazlitt strengthens this conception of Satan, calling him "the most
heroic subject that ever was chosen for a poem" and "the chief
person in his [Milton's] poem." [27] He says that the interest of the
poem arises from Satan's "daring ambition and fierce passions,"
whereas the fall of Adam and Eve provides "little action," but
"much repose, and more enjoyment." [28] Concerning Hazlitt's comment that "everywhere Satan is heroic," one wonders whether he
has forgotten him as toad, vulture, and serpent; and when, at the
end, he says nothing of the "Paradise within," but recalls only
Adam's and Eve's being *"driven* out of Paradise, tasting the first
fruits of *bitterness,"* one realizes that the whole dramatic conflict
of *Paradise Lost* has escaped him. Among the poets of the Romantic
Period, Byron glorified Satan in the drama of *Cain;* and Keats, who

[25] *Ibid.,* p. 538.     [26] *Ibid.,* p. 524.
[27] *Lectures on the English Poets,* ed. by his son. (3d ed.; London: John Templeman,
1841), Lecture III, "On Shakespeare and Milton," p. 121.
[28] *Ibid.,* pp. 127–28.

admired and imitated Milton's poetry, found the "dogmas and superstitions" of Milton's philosophy so simple as to be "tolerably understood by one not much advanced in years." [29] "He did not think into the human heart as Wordsworth has done," said Keats. Wordsworth it was who most clearly understood Milton's true importance as a poet and philosopher, but to him, too, Milton was chiefly impressive as a poet of liberty, whose voice England must heed if she was to retain her "inward happiness." Blake's conception of Satan as hero and of Milton as one of the Devil's party without knowing it is too familiar to need discussion.

Victorians, influenced in large measure by the Romanticists, regarded Milton's theology as outmoded and admired him chiefly for his poetry. As an historian, Macaulay is chiefly interested in Milton, the man, and in his actions in defense of liberty.[30] He regrets that in his own day Milton is so little read and that nineteenth-century readers are "utterly insensible" to the "blessings which England has derived from the Revolution." He himself seems more familiar with Milton's prose than with *Paradise Lost*, for after comparing Dante and Milton and defending Milton's treatment of the supernatural, he commends the style of Milton's prose and says that at its best it is as great as that of the "earlier books" of *Paradise Lost*, as if, like so many others, he read the first part of the epic but never studied it as a whole. Bagehot, writing in 1859 on the occasion of the publication of the first volume of Masson's *Life of Milton*, also naturally discusses Milton the man at some length before he turns to *Paradise Lost*.[31] His conception of Milton, like that of Hazlitt and Wordsworth, was of one who (in Hazlitt's words) "lived apart, in the solitude of his own thoughts," [32] and whose goodness (in Bagehot's words) "is austere and withdraws from the world." [33] Proceeding on this false assumption, Bagehot finds that Milton

---

[29] Letter to John Hamilton Reynolds, May 3, 1818.

[30] *Literary Essays Contributed to the Edinburgh Review* (London: Oxford University Press, 1923), pp. 1–50.

[31] *Literary Studies,* ed. Richard Holt Hutton (London: Longmans, Green and Company, 1879), I, 173–220.

[32] Hazlitt, *op. cit.*, p. 109.          [33] Bagehot, *op. cit.*, p. 181.

failed in his intention of "justifying the ways of God to man," apparently because of his ignorance of man and his world and because of his "not very sensitive imagination." [34] The defects that he points out in *Paradise Lost* are already familiar: God is conceived of as finite, and his treatment of man is a kind of "political transaction"; Satan is made strong and the good angels weak; Adam and Eve are insignificant, unequally matched with Satan. Bagehot admires Satan, Eve, and Milton's style of writing, but, as if to demonstrate his incapacity to understand the central idea of *Paradise Lost,* he adds: "Probably no book shows the transition which our theology has made since the middle of the seventeenth century, at once so plainly and so fully. We do not now compose long narratives to 'justify the ways of God to man.' . . . The teaching of the eighteenth century is in the very atmosphere we breathe. . . . The air of the theology is clarified." Bagehot cannot forgive Milton's basing the scheme of the poem on "an offence against positive morality . . . an unexplained injunction of the Supreme Will," which "is no subject . . . for literary art." Surely Bagehot and his contemporaries were far from Puritanism. Similarly, Matthew Arnold's naturalism left him little sympathy for Milton's Puritanism. Because Arnold found the "obsoleteness" of Milton's theology an obstacle to interpretation and understanding by his generation, he recommended that *Paradise Lost* be read piecemeal, for its poetry.[35] Walter Raleigh, writing toward the end of the nineteenth century, found the same difficulties in interpretation and came to his now famous conclusion that *Paradise Lost* is "an imposing monument to dead ideas." [36] This was plainly the attitude of many readers in the nineteenth century and in the early twentieth century as well.

Early twentieth-century criticism of Milton had little, therefore, on which to base a sound verdict as to Milton's purpose or theme in writing *Paradise Lost,* and the first decade gave small promise of any better interpretation than that of the nineteenth century. To

[34] *Ibid.,* p. 208.
[35] *Mixed Essays, Irish Essays, and Others* (New York: Macmillan Company, 1883), pp. 196–202.
[36] *Milton* (London: Edward Arnold, 1913), p. 88.

Mark Pattison in the latter half of the nineteenth century [37] and to E. N. S. Thompson in the early twentieth,[38] *Paradise Lost* was still obsolete as history or theology, but it had a symbolic meaning, that of the conflict of good and evil and the ultimate triumph of the good. Such interpretation is helpful so far as it goes, but by its obvious vagueness and by the narrowness of its scope it gives rise to charges of extraneous matter in the epic that are not valid if a true definition of Milton's theme is achieved. H. W. Peck,[39] in 1914, noted with regret the decline of interest in Milton's great epic and praised Professor Thompson for his attempt to revive interest in it. Professor Peck cautioned the reader, however, against symbolic or allegorical interpretations and added, "I shall attempt to formulate what seems a more comprehensive view of the meaning of Milton's epic." With surprising and refreshing anticipation of present-day insistence on getting back to the author and his times, he said: "The safest method of approach is doubtless the historical one. What did the poem mean to the author and his contemporaries? Then, in the light of their interpretation, what can it mean to us?" However, after examining the *De Doctrina Christiana* and the criticism of *Paradise Lost* by Milton's contemporaries, Professor Peck concluded that *Paradise Lost* is simply an elaboration of the Christianity of Milton's time, the more or less medieval Christianity that George Santayana has called "The Christian Epic" [40] and that is, therefore, obsolete. To Professor Peck's assertion that Milton's theme is just what he says it is in the opening lines of his epic, the reader is likely to ask, And just what does he say? There, of course, is the crux of the whole matter. Because "the thought of *Paradise Lost,* at least for many, can never again be accepted as a literally veracious account of the creation and fall," said Professor Peck, ". . . the poem can probably never again hold quite the place, especially in the popular mind, that it once had." Professor Peck, consequently, did little to revive interest in or to interpret *Paradise Lost,* as he set out to do.

[37] *Milton* (London: Macmillan Company, 1900), pp. 199 ff.
[38] "The Theme of *Paradise Lost,*" PMLA, XXI (1913), 106–20.
[39] "The Theme of *Paradise Lost,*" loc. cit.
[40] *Reason in Religion* (New York: Charles Scribner's Sons, 1905), pp. 92–96.

In 1907 Paul Elmer More, in his essay on "The Theme of *Paradise Lost*," [41] like Professor Peck deplored the fact that Milton's *Paradise Lost* suffers neglect, partly because "the true theme of his poem is not commonly understood." "Sin," he said, "is not the innermost subject of Milton's epic, nor man's disobedience and fall; these are but the tragic shadows cast about the central light. Justification of the ways of God to man is not the true moral of the plot: this and the whole divine drama are merely the poet's means of raising his conception to the highest generalisation. The true theme is Paradise itself." This Paradise, he said, is what all poets have dreamed of: the Golden Age, a kind of Utopia, apparently, in which the deepest desires of the human heart are satisfied. If More had not described this Golden Age as a pastoral retreat, "a sweet refuge of retirement . . . builded for the heart of our fancy," something like the "repose" of Hazlitt, we might be more willing to agree that the theme of *Paradise Lost* is Paradise. However, man, the maker of his own Paradise, is more important in Milton's epic than the place itself, and *retirement* and *retreat* give no sense of the discipline through which man must go to achieve and maintain his Paradise. Milton was too much concerned with grappling with the problem of life in all its phases to create a dream fancy or a place for pastoral retreat. In other words, Milton wished to deal with man's descent from a superhuman Eden "to human life as we know it, and as Milton knew it, of a mingled web, good and ill together." [42]

The numerous present-day misconceptions concerning *Paradise Lost* and its theme prove that the errors of the eighteenth, nineteenth, and early twentieth centuries still persist, along with some new ones, and, for one reason or another, they are often reiterated with a strange kind of fervor. A few years ago, on an "Invitation to Learning" radio program, Allen Tate, Huntington Cairns, and Mark Van Doren agreed that *Paradise Lost* is not first-rate, not nearly so great as the *Iliad,* because Milton's ideas are obsolete, because his treatment of his myth and his universe is so long that it gets in the reader's way, because the question of why Adam and Eve could not

[41] More, *op. cit.*                [42] Stoll, *op. cit.*, p. 208.

eat of the Tree of Knowledge is never answered, and so forth. The
"invitation to learning," therefore, rested on little more than Milton's
craftsmanship and style. T. S. Eliot was, of course, the source of
many of these conclusions in his objections to the "peculiar doctrines
that *Paradise Lost* enshrines" and in his concession that "we can
certainly enjoy the poetry and yet be fully aware of the intellectual
and moral aberrations of the author." [43] For Miss Rose Macaulay's
discovery that *"Paradise Lost* is a pamphlet on many subjects, by
an author whose tremendous imagination penetrates chaos and the
spheres, but never the human soul," [44] it is difficult to find either
basis or source. G. Wilson Knight, in 1939, regarded Milton as a
"Colossus of stone," [45] who in *Paradise Lost* presented "a cosmic
disharmony, which is, indeed, its explicit theme." [46] As a result, he
regarded the poem as "in itself disharmonious and therefore as a
whole artistically fallacious." Nevertheless, only three years later,
amid the terrors of war, he found that this "Colossus of stone" had
"a living voice" that could "point towards understanding of the
inward mechanisms of the British Constitution" and, acting like
an X-ray, could "both record the agony and forecast recovery." [47]
R. W. Chambers, about the same time that Logan Pearsall Smith
published *Milton and His Modern Critics,* set forth the "hostile
movement" of other American and English critics against *Paradise
Lost.*[48] If critics and poets can so misinterpret the epic, it would
surely seem that the historical approach is the only sure one and
that the scholar, rather than the poet or critic, must help us to
determine its meaning.

It was Professor James Holly Hanford's discussion, in 1919, of
"Milton and the Return to Humanism" [49] that gave us the first
real understanding, it seems to me, of the theme of *Paradise Lost.*

---

[43] Eliot, *op. cit.,* p. 35.            [44] McCaulay, *op. cit.,* p. 140.

[45] Knight, *op. cit.,* p. 111.          [46] *Ibid.,* p. 92.

[47] *Chariot of Wrath, the Message of John Milton to Democracy at War* (London:
Faber and Faber, 1942), p. 17.

[48] "Poets and Their Critics: Langland and Milton." Warton Lecture on English
Poetry. *Proceedings of the British Academy,* Vol. XXVII (London: Humphrey Milford,
1941).

[49] *North Carolina Studies in Philology,* XVI (April, 1919), 126–47.

Professor E. A. Greenlaw, in 1917, had already pointed out Milton's humanism in his comparison of Spenser's *Faerie Queene* and *Paradise Lost*,[50] stressing the influence on Milton of Spenser's philosophy, "drawn ultimately from Plato and Aristotle, modified by Renaissance theories of beauty and virtue, and further modified by Milton by the infusion with it of the theological tradition of the Middle Ages as inherited and re-defined by religious thinkers of the sixteenth and seventeenth centuries."[51] But in his definition of Milton's theme as "temperance," Professor Greenlaw limited it unduly and so showed only a part of Milton's purpose. Indeed, instead of emphasizing the "pagan virtue" of temperance, Milton's concern is rather with the Christian virtues of humility and obedience.[52] Professor Hanford, pointing out the growing tendency to stress Milton's humanism, said: "The essential character of that humanism is its assertion of the spiritual dignity of man, its recognition of the degree to which his higher destinies are in his own hands, its repudiation of the claim of his lower nature to control his higher or of any force or agency external to his own mind and will to achieve for him salvation."[53] This humanism Professor Hanford found to be "sharply and irreconcilably at odds with medieval thought." Its purpose was "the study not of God but of man," and it trusted "human reason as well as intuition and revealed truth as the instrument of its knowledge." Professor Hanford did not minimize Milton's Puritan, and therefore medieval,[54] heritage. Milton's convictions concerning God, evil, retribution, salvation are Puritan and also medieval, he said, since the main body of Puritan doctrine is medieval Christianity. But Milton's philosophy, according to Professor Hanford, "is not a theology, but an interpretation of experience,

[50] "A Better Teacher Than Aquinas," *loc. cit.*, 196–217.

[51] "Spenser's Influence on *Paradise Lost*," *Studies in Philology*, XVII (July, 1920), 320–59.

[52] Cf. Stoll, *op. cit.*, p. 227, and Bush, *English Literature in the Earlier Seventeenth Century*, p. 377.

[53] "Milton and the Return to Humanism," *loc. cit.*, p. 143.

[54] Cf. Ralph Barton Perry, *Puritanism and Democracy* (New York: Vanguard Press, 1944), pp. 83–87; J. H. Robinson, *The Mind in the Making* (New York: Harper's, 1921), pp. 123–47; A. C. McGiffert, *Protestant Thought before Kant* (New York: Charles Scribner's Sons, 1916), pp. 145–54.

based on the bed rock of human freedom, and formulated under the guiding influence of the Bible, the ancients, and the thinkers and poets of the preceding generation. . . . *Paradise Lost* is primarily the epic of man's moral struggle." [55] No doubt to some readers Professor Hanford unduly minimized Milton's Puritan faith in man's dependence upon God, but in his emphasis on man's importance as hero of the epic, on man's freedom of choice, and on his attainment of salvation through reason and self-discipline rather than through divine grace alone, Professor Hanford prepared the way for a real understanding of the theme of Milton's epic.[56]

With this humanistic approach to Milton, Professor H. J. C. Grierson, in 1929, seemed to be in complete agreement in his conclusion that "the theme of the poem, in which he sets out his justification of God's ways to men, is not quite the theme of Puritan sermons and treatises. It comes rather from the Humanist side of Milton's mind." [57] However, in explaining the difference between Milton's theme and that of Puritan sermons, Professor Grierson added:

> His subject is not the Eternal and inscrutable Decrees of God, and the salvation of man through the Imputed Righteousness of Christ. It is the warfare of Reason and Passion in Man whom God has created free; the forfeiture of freedom through man's surrender to passion, Adam's too great love for his tempted and erring wife; the restoration of that freedom through the victory over temptation of the perfect Man, the Son of God, but not himself God.

Here the phrase "the forfeiture of freedom through man's surrender to passion" is misleading, for Milton's Adam and Eve never forfeit their freedom and hence by their own "right reason" are able to repent and obey anew. It is God's way with men that they have free will, and no one, not even Christ, can make the choice for them. Later, in his interpretation of the temptation in *Paradise Lost*

---

[55] "Milton and the Return to Humanism," *loc. cit.,* pp. 144–45.
[56] This interpretation is treated at length in his *Milton Handbook* (New York: F. S. Crofts, 1939), pp. 228 ff.     [57] Grierson, *op. cit.,* p. 231.

as one of "transgressing a tabu"[58] and in his inability to see anything heroic in Adam's and Eve's fall and repentance and preparation for life by Michael's narrative, so that the epic falls off in interest,
Professor Grierson seems to me to have missed the theme and,
therefore, the significance of the epic as a whole.

In Milton's prose tracts both Professor William Haller[59] and
Professor Arthur Barker have pointed out evidences of his humanism.
That humanism, says Professor Barker, implied "confidence in the
powers of man, in human reason, in progress, in a temperate freedom
amid profusion—altogether without a place in the thought of his
fellow-pamphleteers."[60] In the case of Milton's prose, however,
Professor Barker found that "while I have tried to keep in view
the constant influence of humanism, the weight of my emphasis
falls inevitably on Puritanism: man's Fall, his natural corruption,
his regeneration through grace, the peculiar privileges of the elect
aristocracy, the Christian liberty of the regenerate." Similarly, of
course, the reader of Milton's epic must be on guard to weigh the
just proportions of Milton's humanism and Puritanism. It must be
kept in mind, however, that to Milton "man's Fall, his natural
corruption, his regeneration through grace" are still possible only
by his own free choice and that Milton explicitly denied the existence
of an "elect aristocracy."[61] Professor Bush, also, in relation to
Milton's prose, has stressed Milton's humanism.[62]

It was inevitable that Milton should break with Calvinism as
Erasmus had broken with Luther. A humanist believing in human
and divine reason could not uphold the depravity of man and
the arbitrary will of an inscrutable God. No ordinance, human
or from heaven, Milton declared in *Tetrachordon,* can bind against

[58] *Milton and Wordsworth* (New York: Macmillan Company, 1937), pp. 119–20.
[59] William Haller, *The Rise of Puritanism* (New York: Columbia University Press,
1938), pp. 348 ff., and *Tracts on Liberty in the Puritan Revolution* (New York:
Columbia University Press, 1934), pp. 420–22.
[60] Arthur Barker, *Milton and the Puritan Dilemma* (Toronto: Toronto University
Press, 1942), Intro., pp. xiv ff.
[61] Cf. Maurice Kelley, "The Theological Dogma of *Paradise Lost,* III, 173–202,"
*PMLA,* LII (March, 1937), 75–79.
[62] *English Literature in the Earlier Seventeenth Century,* pp. 376–77.

the good of man. And in the tracts on divorce, in *Areopagitica,* and most fully and explicitly in the *Christian Doctrine,* Milton evolved that enlarged conception of Christian liberty of which he was in his day the great exponent . . . for Milton as for Hooker and Taylor and other Christian humanists the law of God is the law of right reason and of nature.

As Milton himself says in the *Areopagitica:* "When God gave him [Adam] reason, he gave him freedom to choose, for reason is but choosing . . . This justifies the high providence of God."

There are several reasons why, it seems to me, the theme of *Paradise Lost* may be concisely stated as "the making of the greater man," and in the following paragraphs I shall try to show why that interpretation satisfies the demands of the whole epic rather than one or another part of it.

In the first place, there is general agreement among scholars today concerning Milton's choice of man as a theme for his epic. Professor Merritt Y. Hughes, in his edition of *Paradise Lost,* wrote as follows: "In *Man's Disobedience* Milton saw a finer subject than Achilles' wrath and in the *greater Man,* Christ, a better ideal than Renaissance critics recognized in Ulysses. Like George Chapman, he thought that the word 'man' in the first line of the *Odyssey* announced that epic as an ideal human portrait." [63] Professor Tillyard, though finding it "difficult to attach any one broad meaning to the poem," [64] nevertheless concluded that "everything was meant to be subordinate to the human drama." [65] Professor Barker, discussing Milton's prose tracts, said: "He wrote of man's destiny with eloquence and profound conviction at a time when the democratic theory of society was receiving its first practical formulation." [66] If, as is generally conceded, the spirit of Milton's prose persists in his epic, we may conclude that his concern in verse as well as in prose was "man's destiny." To Professor R. W. Chambers the theme of the epic was "man's fortitude" in a conflict with "the most dread

[63] Garden City: Doubleday, Doran, 1935, p. 8, n. 4.
[64] Tillyard, *op. cit.,* p. 295.          [65] *Ibid.,* p. 257.
[66] Barker, *op. cit.,* Intro., p. xiv.

antagonist ever conceived." [67] And, as I have indicated, Professor
Bush stresses Milton's "profound concern with 'man, the heart of
man, and human life.' " [68] John Diekhoff says: "Nevertheless it is
Adam and Eve who are important. They are the central characters
in the poem." [69] The list of such corroborations could be much
extended, but perhaps these statements will serve to indicate the
general agreement among scholars as to Milton's intent to write
an epic of man, rather than of Satan or God.

In the second place, so far as Milton was concerned, the term
*the greater Man* was by no means limited to Christ. To him all
mankind were "sons of God," [70] capable of becoming better, nobler
beings. Being both humanist and Puritan, Milton had faith in
Man's potential goodness and in the ideal possibilities which his
divine origin should give him. From the days of the Seventh Prolusion to *Samson Agonistes* he dreamed and wrote of the "labour
of high soaring" for which man was created and endowed. With
time, indeed, Milton, like some of his contemporaries, became a
perfectibilitarian, confident of man's ability to attain the perfection
that the Gospel "proposes" but that is "not to be required." [71] The
adjurations of Christ, "Be ye perfect, even as your Father in Heaven
is perfect," [72] and of the apostle Paul to the Corinthians, "Be perfect," [73] no doubt meant to Milton exactly what they said. For he
speaks of Adam and Eve as "perfet within"; [74] Raphael tells Adam
that "God made thee perfet"; [75] Noah is said to be "so perfet and
so just" [76] that God decides to raise another world after the flood;
Abraham is "one faithful man" [77] from whom a nation was to

[67] "Poets and Their Critics: Langland and Milton," *loc. cit.,* pp. 25, 30.
[68] *Paradise Lost in Our Time,* p. 27.
[69] *Milton's Paradise Lost, a Commentary on the Argument* (New York: Columbia
University Press, 1946), p. 49.
[70] Cf. Alden Sampson, *Studies in Milton* (New York: Moffat, Yard and Company,
1913), pp. 196–97, 232; also *Paradise Lost,* Book III, l. 151, and *Paradise Regained,*
Book IV, ll. 197, 520.
[71] *The Student's Milton,* ed. F. A. Patterson (New York: F. S. Crofts and Company,
1930), pp. 613, 615, 996, 1050.
[72] Matthew 5:48.        [73] II Corinthians 13:11.        [74] Book VIII, l. 642.
[75] Book V, l. 524.        [76] Book XI, l. 876, from Genesis 6:9.
[77] Book XII, l. 113, from Genesis 17:1: "The Lord . . . said unto him [Abraham]
'. . . walk before me, and be thou perfect.' "

spring by which all nations were to be blessed; Isaac and Jacob, like Abraham, were distinguished "in faith, in wisdom, and renown"; [78] Enoch is "that just man" [79] whom Heaven rescues from impious hands; Moses is "Mediator," [80] much as Christ is later; Christ is called "second Adam"; [81] Mary is "second Eve"; [82] both Adam and Eve are described as having "looks Divine," or "Divine resemblance," [83] and in his sonnet on his blindness Milton missed the sight of the "human face divine." Man's capacity for excellence Milton further asserts in his *Tractate on Education* where he defines the end of learning as "possessing our souls of true virtue, which being united to the heavenly grace of faith, makes up the highest perfection." This doctrine of human excellence, which persists throughout the history of human thought, in Milton's time became a moot question with Luther and Calvin denying man perfection in this life, except by imputation. Milton's own position is clear, it seems to me, from his prose works as well as from *Paradise Lost,* and having traced the development of that attitude in another study, I will not dwell on it longer here.

In his belief in the perfectibility and divinity of human beings, Milton plainly breaks with the medieval doctrine of original sin and total depravity, which the reformers, Luther, Calvin, and Zwingli, held and which persisted to the end of the seventeenth century and beyond. "Man is utterly corrupt and depraved," said Calvin, "and humility alone becomes him in the presence of God." [84] This belief in the "nothingness of man and the overmastering power of God," [85] which was "so central and pervasive as to contaminate every natural impulse, every human faculty, and every social or creative achievement," [86] is not entirely foreign to our own time, as we sometimes discover to our sad surprise. Recently I heard a Protestant doctor of divinity say in a sermon: "It is unseemly to ascribe great merit to any mortal." In the midst of World War II,

[78] Book XII, l. 154, from Genesis 22:18.
[79] Book XI, l. 681, from Genesis 5:24.
[80] Book XII, l. 240.                    [81] Book V, l. 387.
[82] Book IV, l. 291.                     [83] Book III, l. 44.
[84] *Institutes* (ed. 1559), Book I, chap. i, sec. 2.
[85] McGiffert, *op. cit.*, p. 86.         [86] *Ibid.*, p. 84.

when many mortals were showing merits such as the world had never seen, the statement seemed startling in the extreme. This belittling stress on man's human limitations Milton seems to rebel against throughout his life. To him, apparently, the way to produce finer human beings is not to belittle them but rather to insist on their divine origin, their great capacities for intellectual and spiritual development, and, above all, their ability, in the light of knowledge and right reason, to know and love and obey and humbly walk with God. Such men are "greater men," well on their way toward "perfection." But there are other greater men as well: those who, having fallen, repent and regain right reason and are restored to their oneness with God. To Milton such men are indeed even greater men than those who have never known the awfulness of evil, for theirs is no longer the "fugitive and cloistered virtue" of untested innocence, and out of evil they have made good. Adam, at the close of *Paradise Lost,* is such a "greater man," for he, too, has "regained Paradise" and thus restored the possibility of happiness for all mankind. Samson is another such "greater man," for he, too, having fallen, rose to heroic heights of love and obedience, in a drama that Dr. Johnson said had a beginning and an end but no middle, but whose all-important middle actually shows the making of the greater man and thus makes compatible the beginning and the end. Milton himself, from many points of view, was just such a "greater man." All his life, by strict self-discipline, he sought to be the greater man whom he analyzed for others. The vision he sets forth in his Seventh Prolusion of the heights to which the human mind and character can attain shows the ardor of his convictions while still in the University.[87] Each succeeding work—the sonnets, *Comus, Lycidas,* the prose passages relating to himself—shows his increasing concern for living as he conceived a great poet must live: to sway men, to be a great teacher, to influence others to become "greater men." Perhaps in no place is Milton's respect for humankind so obvious as in his assertion of his purpose to "justify the ways of God to

[87] Cf. Phyllis B. and E. M. W. Tillyard, eds., *Milton's Private Correspondence and Academic Exercises* (Cambridge, [Eng.]: University Press, 1932), Intro., pp. xxxiii–xxxix, and Prolusion, pp. 111–15.

man," a purpose no medieval writer would have thought of asserting, or would have dared to assert. Nor did Milton fail to see greater
men and women about him in his own day, as his sonnets to Cromwell, Lord Fairfax, Sir Henry Vane, Henry Lawes, Lady Margaret
Ley, and others show.

The "one greater Man" referred to in the fourth line of *Paradise
Lost,* who is to "restore us" and "regain the blissful Seat" of Paradise,
is undoubtedly Christ, but by the time *Paradise Lost* was written,
nothing was clearer than the need of other greater men, to whom
the life of Christ would serve as a goal or a pattern. Salvation was
not something to be forced on mankind; "for," says Milton, "if
our personal religion were not in some degree dependent on our-
selves, and in our own power, God could not properly enter into
a covenant with us; neither could we perform, much less swear to
perform, the conditions of that covenant." [88] A "second Adam" was
impossible without a first Adam, and Adam's, that is, mankind's,
discovery of a paradise within that was happier far was a necessary
preparation for the recovery of an earthly paradise by a second
Adam. Only so was God assured that man could and would be
ready for a second Adam.

In the very epithet "the second Adam" Milton shows, of course,
his sense of pride and gratification in the humanity of Christ, an
attitude most clearly shown in *Paradise Regained.* There Christ
himself, tempted as sorely as were Adam and Eve, became "a greater
man," though he did so by choosing good instead of evil and so
never lost true happiness. Milton's comparison of Christ with
Hercules [89] and Christ's modest comparison of himself with such
ancients as Socrates,[90] Quintius, Fabricius, Curius, Regulus,[91] as
well as the human traits of Christ taken from the Gospels and his
return in the end to his humble lot in Nazareth, all reveal Milton's
admiration for the life and character of Christ, the man. It is not
surprising, therefore, in *Paradise Regained,* that Christ, like Milton,
prefers the true fame that comes only "when God, looking on the

[88] *De Doctrina Christiana,* chap. xii, *The Student's Milton,* p. 1,000.
[89] Book IV, l. 562.      [90] Book III, ll. 97–99.      [91] Book II, l. 446.

Earth, with approbation marks the just man," [92] or in the *De Doctrina Christiana,* in his analysis of "The Son of God" and elsewhere,[93] Milton stresses the human side of the Son and his dependence on God, the Father. To the Puritans "this humanization of God is not a degradation . . . his humanity is the same thing as the divinity of man, both consisting in the victory of the will over temptation." [94] Man's divine origin, his reflection of the divine image, his capacity for truth and goodness gave him ideal possibilities, even to a state of ultimate "perfection," and the greater men of *Paradise Lost* have shown their ability to use those possibilities and have made humankind worth saving. If it were not worth saving, there would have been no need for the "second Adam."

The development of Adam and Eve to greater man and woman involves their becoming moral agents. They freely choose to know both good and evil, to succumb to the "hybris" of desire, to lose happiness, but with the help of God's mercy they also choose to learn again "to pray, repent, and bring obedience due," and finally they achieve the "Paradise within thee, happier far." It is to this Adam and Eve that Michael is able to say: "Thou hast attained the sum of wisdom." [95] If such an achievement seems unheroic or if such a conclusion makes possible "a falling off of interest in the later books," [96] it is difficult to think of how the poem or its theme could be more heroic or more profoundly interesting. Nor do the last books seem pessimistic, with an "unadmitted pessimism, which also affects the unity." [97] If Adam and Eve have become greater human beings, "with all the world before them," surely there is hope, not pessimism. Like *Samson Agonistes, Paradise Lost,* it seems to me, concludes with such grandeur and significance as to make

[92] Book III, ll. 60–62.

[93] Chapter v, "The Son of God," pp. 944 ff., and chap. vii, "Of the Creation," *The Student's Milton,* p. 981, where Milton says: "Nevertheless, even he [Christ] is called *the seed of the woman, the seed of David according to the flesh;* that is, undoubtedly, according to his human nature. There seems therefore no reason, why the soul of man should be made an exception to the general law of creation."

[94] Perry, *op. cit.,* p. 278.          [95] Book XII, l. 575.

[96] Grierson, *Milton and Wordsworth,* p. 119.

[97] E. M. W. Tillyard, *Milton,* p. 291.

Books I and II, the books usually called best by those who have read no further, seem mild by comparison.

In the development of Adam and Eve as moral agents, *Paradise Lost* introduces much learning, the "unnecessary ostentation of learning," to which Addison objected, the lengthy treatment of the myth and the universe to which Allen Tate objected because it "gets in the reader's way." The theme of "the making of the greater man," however, involves Milton's introduction of learning or knowledge, since it is by learning that Adam and Eve become able to exercise right reason or conscience and hence as moral agents to choose good rather than evil.[98] It is not difficult to see why, historically, Milton should have defended learning so valiantly throughout his life, from his Seventh Prolusion to *Samson Agonistes,* although it is in his prose works that he most consistently praises all learning in general and in his three major works that he clearly sets knowledge of the Bible and Christian doctrine above all other learning.[99] In his defense of learning Milton again broke with the Middle Ages; for it was also a medieval characteristic to dwell on man's profound ignorance as compared with God's omniscience, his incapacity to know more than the Church saw fit to teach, and the dangers that beset the path of one who tried to know more than he was supposed to know. It was in this vein that Dante wrote of Ulysses, who, though a hero to the ancients, to the Middle Ages became a symbol of ungodly seeking after forbidden knowledge. Sailing foolishly beyond the Straits of Gibraltar, his ship was caught in a whirlpool and destroyed, as it should properly have been. Thus Dante showed how the thirst for knowledge and the passion for discovery are punished by divine power.[100] Similarly in Sebastian Brant's *Ship of Fools,* at the close

---

[98] Cf. *Paradise Lost,* Book V, ll. 507–12.

[99] Cf. especially *ibid.,* Book VII, ll. 118–30, Book VIII, ll. 159–97, and *Paradise Regained,* Book IV, ll. 285–364. Though these passages seem to repudiate classical learning, Milton rather gives it its due place as helpful in the understanding of the Word of God and the Holy Spirit, but not of equal authority. Cf. Bush, *English Literature in the Earlier Seventeenth Century,* pp. 377–79.

[100] *Inferno,* Canto XXVI, ll. 90–142. Cf. Karl Vossler, *Medieval Culture: an Introduction to Dante and His Times* (New York: Harcourt, Brace and Company, 1929), II, 281–83.

of the Middle Ages, the voyage of Columbus is deplored as evidence
of man's sinfulness in seeking to go beyond the known world; and
there are many such examples. With the Renaissance, this attitude,
of course, gave way to the demand for a revival and an advancement
of learning. As if to put an end to the medieval attitude forever,
Bacon had printed on the title page of his *Advancement of Learning*
a picture of a ship sailing boldly past Hercules' Pillars, guarding the
Straits of Gibraltar, and out into the unknown sea beyond. Nevertheless, in Bacon's brave insistence that "there is no danger at all
in the proportion or quantity of knowledge, how large soever" [101]
and in his stirring plea for extending the horizons of knowledge on
every hand, even he reveals some of the fear of pride in learning
that remained as a part of the medieval inheritance of Puritanism.[102]
A fundamental tenet of the Christian Epic was its belief in the
necessity of complete humility as a condition of man's reconciliation
with God. Therefore, whereas the pagan world could find relief
from its passions and its pessimism in learning, to the Puritan "the
seeming self-sufficiency of the sage was deemed the last stronghold
of pride, which must be surrendered to faith," [103] before man could
be saved. This was Bacon's interpretation also: "But it was the
proud knowledge of good and evil, with an intent in man to give
law unto himself, and to depend no more upon God's commandments, which was the form of the temptation." [104] This "proud
knowledge," says Bacon, "is not the natural knowledge of creatures"
or of the universe, all of which is good—as Adam learns, also, from
Raphael in *Paradise Lost*.

In Bacon's and Milton's time, there was another reason for the
questioning of the goodness of power through knowledge which
the buoyant optimism of the Renaissance promised. The Renaissance,
which gave men a new and increased respect and desire for learning,
later inspired a fear lest man lose hold of God and the eternal
verities. The new theories as to the structure of the universe, whereby
man became a mere speck on the surface of one of the planets,

---

[101] Everyman Edition (London: J. M. Dent and Sons, n. d.), pp. 5–6.
[102] Perry, *op. cit.*, p. 85.        [103] *Ibid.*        [104] Everyman Edition, p. 5.

also stirred new doubts and fears. Late sixteenth-century and early seventeenth-century disillusion, therefore, is not hard to find, in such works as Donne's *Anniversaries,* Sir John Davies' *Nosce Teipsum,* Sir Thomas Browne's *Religio Medici,* and others, as they voiced their concern lest new discoveries might be nothing more than new kinds of error or that all their new learning might bring only new sorrows. In this questioning Milton, like Bacon, no doubt shared. Both saw in learning a power that would enable mankind, not only to perform well their private and public duties and thus exert an influence for good on their own time, but also to know God aright and to be like Him. As Milton put it in his *Tractate on Education:* "The end of learning is to repair the ruins of our first parents by regaining to know God aright and out of that knowledge to love him, to be like him." [105] Nevertheless, both Bacon and Milton realized the danger that man's trying to know God and be like Him involved the temptation to feel equal to God and therefore independent of Him and free from obedience to His laws. Such "hybris" or "pride" would prevent the repentance and faith necessary to return to happiness in a knowledge of God's laws and obedience to them. Learning alone, then, though a powerful aid, could never make a greater man—it must be coupled with man's sense of and choice of humble dependence upon God.

Milton's careful distinction, in *Paradise Lost,* between useful and useless knowledge and between moral and immoral knowledge is, therefore, no mere "ostentation of learning," but an important factor in his plan for making greater men. Since, from time immemorial, the word *knowledge* or *to know* has included the idea of concupiscence,[106] and since the idea that evil originated in sexual sin has influenced all succeeding theories concerning knowledge, Milton's reasons for choosing the story of Adam and Eve to show knowledge that is good and knowledge that is evil are obvious. Eve fell through desire for power through knowledge, and Adam fell

[105] *The Student's Milton,* p. 726.
[106] Cf. Norman Powell Williams, *The Ideas of the Fall and of Original Sin* (London: Longmans, Green, 1927), p. 34.

through weakness of will, but both sinned through inordinate sexual desire, the "sign and seal," according to Augustine, "of human abasement." [107] Their fall, which resulted from an overweening sense of superiority to God's laws, was a sin which, to Milton, included all the rest: "For what sin can be named, which was not included in this act?" [108] Their immoral use of knowledge, however, in no way disturbed the goodness of learning itself, and so Milton shows them being taught, by Raphael in their state of innocence and by Michael in their state of regeneration, all that they need to know. Such knowledge they needed, to know God aright and thus to preserve their liberty and happiness.[109] When, therefore, in *Paradise Lost* and in *Paradise Regained,* Milton seems to repudiate the admiration and desire for boundless knowledge that he expressed in the Seventh Prolusion,[110] he does so, it seems to me, only to stress again his belief that the purpose of all learning is to know God and that if learning fails to reveal God and His laws, it is useless. Knowing God and His laws and His universe, according to Milton, will help man to enjoy true happiness by enabling him to avoid the dangers involved in liberty. Freedom of choice, by its very nature, depends on knowledge. Nowhere, therefore, does Milton repudiate his faith in the need of learning, though of course the *Areopagitica* is his most complete avowal of that faith. There "the fruits which a dull ease and cessation of our knowledge will bring forth among the people" are properly deplored; whereas the "dignity of Learning," the "glorious ways of Truth and prosperous

---

[107] Cf. J. H. Robinson, *The Mind in the Making* (New York and London: Harper's, 1921), pp. 139-41.

[108] *De Doctrina Christiana,* chap. xi, "Of the Fall of Our First Parents, and of Sin," *The Student's Milton,* p. 997.

[109] Cf. J. H. Hanford, "The Temptation Motive in Milton," *Studies in Philology,* XV (1918), 178-79, and Murray W. Bundy, "Milton's View of Education in *Paradise Lost," Journal of English and Germanic Philology,* XXI (1922), 127.

[110] In this connection Professor Bush's admirable discussion of Milton's stress on temperance in learning, *Paradise Lost in Our Time,* pp. 50 ff., should be read. See also G. F. Sensabaugh, "Milton on Learning," *Studies in Philology,* XLIII (April, 1946), 258-72, on the change in Milton's attitude toward learning from the days of his *Tractate* and *Areopagitica* to those of *Paradise Lost.* There is less change, however, than is generally supposed.

virtue," are duly praised as England's means to "true liberty" and happiness. There the parochial minister who is "at his Hercules pillars in a warm benefice," who fears lest a new book be published and he may have to read it, is properly denounced; whereas the man who "hath been labouring the hardest labour in the deep mines of knowledge" is lauded as a soldier in the war for Truth. There Milton glories in the fact that men have "minds that can wander beyond all limit and satiety. . . . For who knows not that Truth is strong next to the Almighty?" [111]

Milton's aim to show how a greater man is made was undoubtedly a part of the learning he acquired from his teacher Spenser, whom he called a "better teacher than Scotus or Aquinas." For in "fashioning a gentleman," a phrase full of meaning in the sixteenth century if not today, Spenser was actually setting forth his idea of the art of right living.[112] Being a humanist like Milton, he, too, chose the theme of "ideal humanity." [113] What has been said of Spenser's art applies equally well to Milton's:

> He dedicates his art not to the glory of God but to the praise of the godlike in man, grounding his ethic upon self-knowledge and self-mastery rather than upon abstract righteousness or fear of the Lord. So his ideal is no Calvinistic theocracy but a kingdom of this world. . . . To aid the working of universal law is the high prerogative of man. Endowed with reason and free-will he is master of his fate, clearing his way towards the highest good. If he fail, the fault is not in his stars nor in divine predestination, but in himself. If he succeed, virtue proves its own reward. The true hero who has gained the mastery over reason and appetite will pursue wisdom and beauty wherever they may be found.

[111] *The Student's Milton*, pp. 747 and 751. Cf. also the autobiographic passage opening Book II of *The Reason of Church Government Urged against Prelaty*, in which he admits that knowledge is a responsibility, but one that he proposes to use for the furtherance of truth.

[112] Cf. B. E. C. Davis, *Edmund Spenser* (Cambridge, [Eng.]: University Press, 1933), p. 62. Earlier Professor Greenlaw also pointed out, in "A Better Teacher than Aquinas," *loc. cit.*, p. 204, that Spenser's purpose, in his allegories of Redcrosse and Guyon, was to show "the growth of the soul toward perfection."

[113] Davis, *op. cit.*, p. 68.

. . . So Nature enjoins no blind acceptance of theological dogma nor the sacrifice of present reality to an unknown future, but a sense of responsibility, conformity with the law of self-development whereby every creature, fulfilling its destiny, may further the realization of divine purpose.[114]

Spenser's, like Milton's, was a Christian humanism, but it remained for Milton to stress with new force the values of a knowledge of God and of obedience to the laws of the universe.

The true dignity of man seemed to Milton, in the seventeenth century, to be "degenerately forgotten."[115] Nothing was more timely, therefore, than his efforts to restore that dignity, in prose and in verse and in his own arduous pursuit of what he considered the highest good. If his own age had forgotten the bases of true liberty and happiness, then he intended to help restore man to his natural dignity by setting forth the need of greater men and the means whereby greater men could be developed. The "proud knowledge" of succeeding ages has obscured the magnificence of his achievement. In our own day, a proud self-sufficiency in some needless learning as well as some new and profoundly harmful knowledge may destroy the human race—unless the old lesson of humility and faith and obedience can be learned anew. God's laws, according to Milton, cannot be violated with impunity. The only assurance that they will not be violated lies in the constant development of such greater men and women as Milton defined for us in *Paradise Lost*.

[114] *Ibid.*, pp. 242–43.
[115] *Tetrachordon*, opening exposition on Genesis 1:27: "So God created man in his own image," *The Student's Milton*, p. 652.

# MILTON AND THE IDEA OF
# PERFECTION

THE IDEA of perfection has been an important concept in the philosophical and religious thought of all ages and all peoples. It seems, like morality, to be implicit in life itself. There is no history of the idea, but several studies of its occurrence, in its oriental, classical, medieval, and modern forms, make apparent its universality.[1] The *Li Ki* of the Chinese, conceived of as "the complete and natural discharge of all duties"; the *teleos* of Aristotle, of which he says in his *Metaphysics:* "Things are complete in virtue of having attained their end"; the translation of *teleos* into the Latin *perfectio,* meaning "completion," but used later to describe a state of excellence both human and divine throughout the history of Christian theology—all these forms of the idea of perfection have certain traits in common as well as their own specific differences. That the idea of perfection was much discussed in Milton's day, when so many controversial issues were struggling for expression and solution, is easy to understand, and his own frequent use of the terms *perfect* and *perfection* [2] shows his concern for an accurate interpretation of the concept. It is the purpose of this paper to study his use of the term, in both prose and poetry, in an effort to determine the meaning it had for

[1] Cf. Frederic Platt, "Perfection," *Encyclopedia of Religion and Ethics,* ed. James Hastings (New York: Charles Scribner's Sons, 1917), IX, 727–37; R. Newton Flew, *The Idea of Perfection in Christian Theology* (London: Oxford University Press, 1934); Martin Foss, *The Idea of Perfection in the Western World* (Princeton: Princeton University Press, 1946); Radoslav A. Tsanoff, "The Notion of Perfection," *The Philosophical Review,* XLIX (January, 1940), 25–36; R. Garrigou-Lagrange, *Christian Perfection and Contemplation,* transl. Sister M. Timothea Doyle (St. Louis: B. Herder Book Company, 1946). Dr. Flew's Preface cites other studies written from Wesleyan, Catholic, or other perfectionist viewpoints.

[2] Bradshaw's *Concordance to the Poetical Works* and the Index to the Columbia Edition of *The Works of John Milton* (New York: Columbia University Press, 1931) provide exact references.

him and any changes in meaning that may have occurred in the course of time. Such a study sheds considerable light in each case on the context in which the term occurs and on Milton's relations to others of his day who were dealing with the same problem. The fact that the idea of perfection has had so great a significance in the history of philosophy and religion and such a profound effect on human life and achievement in every field of endeavor makes essential, to the student of literature and particularly to the student of Milton, some understanding of its meaning and history.

As one whose mind "had ranged through the whole realm of speculation," from "ancient philosophy, Biblical and Patristic thought, Reformation theology in all its varieties," to the "philosophic movements and religious heterodoxies of his own day," [3] Milton reveals, in his agreements and disagreements concerning the idea of perfection, the concepts of most of the other theorists preceding him and contemporary with him. To the reader who thinks of him chiefly as a humanist, his interpretation of the idea of perfection may seem to be purely classical or Platonist, and at times it is. To the reader who thinks of him as a Christian humanist, however, the numerous instances of Christian influence on his definition of perfection are ample evidence of the great gulf between his interpretation and that of the ancients. In other words, the Bible, Milton's chief authority, stands between; and Milton, like his contemporaries, has new meanings.

Briefly, the chief difference between the Greek and the Christian ideas of perfection is that one is static and the other dynamic; the one means completion, and the other implies life and growth. To the Greeks, perfection meant achievement of a set purpose or attainment of an end, later restated by Thomas Aquinas, in one of his definitions of perfection, as follows: "Perfectio consistit in hoc quod pertingat ad finem." [4] In the realm of things, such a definition is applicable and understandable. It is easy to conceive of a perfect

[3] James Holly Hanford, *A Milton Handbook* (New York: F. S. Crofts and Company, 1939), p. 235.

[4] *Summa*, IIa. IIae. q. 184, a. 1. Quoted by Foss, *op. cit.*, p. 8 n.

tool, a perfect phrase, or a perfect skill in the performance of a task. It is when the word enters the realm of human beings and of the Deity, where there are no preconceived ideas of purpose or end, that it seems no longer applicable. Moreover, it is logically impossible to conceive of degrees of perfection or completion; hence the conception of God as highest perfection and man as of a higher perfection than animals or things is illogical. For centuries, therefore, the Greeks accepted the limitation of the term *perfection* to the idea of completeness of things, of the mechanization of life into a system of fixed objects, which later influenced Descartes, Spinoza, and Hobbes and led in Milton's time to Cartesian dualism and Hobbes' materialism. To Plato and Aristotle and to their contemporaries, however, this limitation of the idea of perfection was intolerable. Through their concepts of *Being* [5] and *Becoming* [6] and of God as "the aim which aims at itself," [7] they pushed out the boundaries of the meaning of perfection in such a way as to make possible the paradoxical reconciliation by Thomas Aquinas of the finite and mechanistic conception of completion with the infinite and spiritual conceptions of Christianity.

Illogical though it may be in its new surroundings, the philosophical term *perfection* entered the realm of religion and has remained there ever since. The Bible, under Greek influence, uses the term frequently in both Old and New Testaments, as any good concordance reveals. The New Testament refers to God, man, and things as *perfect*. The Old Testament, however, never refers to God as *perfect,* and in its numerous uses of the term concerning things or man, it preserves its original meaning of "completeness." The perfection of beauty, of counsel, of the temple, and so forth is clearly that of meeting a standard or achieving an end. Even in its description of man, it has practically the same meaning, for it expresses God's idea (that is, man's conception of God's idea) of a completeness that man has or has not met. Noah, for example, is called "a just man and perfect in his generations"; [8] Abraham is

---

[5] Foss, *op. cit.*, p. 15.    [6] *Ibid.*, pp. 17–18.    [7] *Ibid.*, p. 19.
[8] Genesis 6:9.

commanded by God to "walk before me, and be thou perfect"; [9] Moses commands the Israelites to "be perfect with the Lord thy God"; [10] Job is called "perfect and upright," [11] though he himself, in his torment, says, "If I say I am perfect, it shall also prove me perverse. Though I were perfect, yet would I not know my soul. . . . He [God] destroyeth the perfect and the wicked"; [12] the Psalmist sings, "I will behave myself wisely in a perfect way"; [13] and the people of Tyre are called "perfect in thy ways" until iniquity overcomes them.[14] The Psalmist also sings of God's "perfect way," [15] but of God's own "completeness" the Old Testament never speaks. "It is by no means accidental," says Professor Martin Foss, "that the Jewish philosophers, whose adoration of the old God was stronger than the strongest Greek influence, very seldom surrendered to the ideal of divine perfection." [16] Philo, Maimonides, and others maintained that the Living God is beyond knowledge and therefore beyond perfection.

For the New Testament writers, however, the term *perfection* has clearly taken on a new meaning, that of Excellence, which, in a sense, is the exact opposite of the idea of completion. Now, instead of "beyondlessness," it means that which is beyond; instead of implying limitations, it expresses the surmounting of those limitations. The idea of degrees of perfection is also incorporated; and perfectibility implies "a never ending excelling movement." [17] God now becomes supreme goodness, whose excellence has no limits because there is no one to set any limits. In the New Testament, therefore, Milton found Christ's well-known and surprising adjuration: "Be ye therefore perfect, even as your Father which is in heaven is perfect." [18] He also found Paul's farewell command to the people of Corinth: "Be perfect," [19] as well as his reference to the time when the Ephesians should attain unto "a perfect man," [20] or when the Colossians should "stand perfect and complete in all the will of God," [21] or when the Hebrews were to "Make you perfect in every

[9] Genesis 17:1.  
[10] Deuteronomy 18:13.  
[11] Job 1:1.  
[12] Job 9:20–22.  
[13] Psalms 101:2.  
[14] Ezekiel 28:30.  
[15] Psalms 18:30.  
[16] Foss, *op. cit.*, p. 29.  
[17] *Ibid.*, p. 32.  
[18] Matthew 5:48.  
[19] I Corinthians 13:11.  
[20] Ephesians 4:12.  
[21] Colossians 4:12.

good work to do his will." [22] He found references, also, to Christ as "the captain of their salvation made perfect through suffering"; [23] or as one who "being made perfect, he became the author of eternal salvation unto all them that obey him." [24] James is told that "If any man offend not in word, the same is a perfect man"; [25] Peter is told to "make you perfect"; [26] John is told that "as he [God] is, so are we in this world . . . made perfect" in love.[27] Numerous other uses of the terms *perfect* and *perfection* in the Bible, as well as in the commentaries of the Church Fathers, the Reformers, Arminius, and the Cambridge Platonists before Milton's time and in the beliefs of the sects of his own time, gave Milton ample reason for thoughtful consideration of the problem of perfection, as his works testify.

What were the ideas concerning perfection of such interpreters as Augustine, Thomas Aquinas, Luther, Calvin, Melancthon, Arminius, the Cambridge Platonists—Henry More, John Smith, Benjamin Whichcote, and their friends—and finally the despised and persecuted sects, whose search for truth the Renaissance humanist Robert Greville, Lord Brooke, interpreted and defended and whose opinions and demands influenced Milton more than we realize? [28] Milton's

[22] Hebrews 13:21.          [23] Hebrews 2:10.          [24] Hebrews 5:9.
[25] James 3:2.              [26] I Peter 5:10.          [27] I John 4:17.
[28] Cf. William Haller, *Tracts on Liberty in the Puritan Revolution* (New York: Columbia University Press, 1934), I, 20–22; David Masson, *Life and Times of John Milton* (London: Macmillan Company, 1859–94), VI, 682–83; James Holly Hanford, *op. cit.*, p. 237; Don M. Wolfe, *Milton in the Puritan Revolution* (New York: Thomas Nelson and Sons, 1941), pp. 51–66; Alden Sampson, *Studies in Milton* (New York: Moffat, Yard and Company, 1913), pp. 167 ff. Milton's commendation of Lord Brooke's tract on the *Nature of Truth* (*Areopagitica*, Columbia Edition of *The Works of John Milton*, IV, 346) included approval of Brooke's plea to "hear with patience and humility those, however they be miscall'd, that desire to live purely, in such a use of Gods Ordinances, as the best guidance of their conscience gives them." Of Milton's praise of Lord Brooke's defense of the sects, Professor Haller says (*op. cit.*, p. 22): "He [Milton], too, felt the appeal of those notions of the sects which, stripped of extravagance, spoke to him of light and love, of truth shining in all men's breasts and uniting them by reason and discourse one with another." Professor Hanford says (*op. cit.*, p. 237): "His religious and political sympathies were on the side of the independent sects . . . in the seventeenth century." Don Wolfe summarizes Milton's position as follows (*op. cit.*, pp. 61 and 66): "Except for antinomianism, Milton's sectarian position combined planks from most of the heretical platforms of his day. . . . Milton was one with the nucleus of enlightened and determined sectarians." Masson specifies

idea of the relative authority of the earliest commentators is apparent throughout his writings. Nowhere are we left in doubt of the prime authority of the Bible. He deplores the fact that "we leave the Bible to gadde after these traditions of the ancients," [29] while the ancients themselves, Augustine and others, confess that their knowledge was only what they had gathered from the Bible. "Nothing," he says, can be to us Catholic or universal in Religion, but what the Scripture teaches"; [30] and again: "The Scripture is our only Principle in Religion." [31] Nevertheless, it was with the Church Fathers that the new interpretation of perfection began; and it was they who raised such new questions as whether Christian perfection implies a state of sinlessness; whether it is possible of attainment in this life; whether it is to be attained by man's own efforts or only imputed to him by the grace of God; whether it depends on faith alone or on faith and works and love; and whether it is attained by degrees, so that one may conceive of perfect, more perfect, most perfect states of being, even up to "the infinite excellence" which "constitutes the true perfection of God." [32] To all of these problems Milton, too, at one time or another, turned his attention and found his own solutions. In the study of his solutions, it is interesting to note how he pondered the problems, at times weighing the evidence as if not wholly certain and at other times speaking firmly and with conviction. Plainly his conclusions did not remain fixed and unchanged, but were modified with time and with increased knowledge.

Among the early Church Fathers, Clement of Rome, whose two Epistles to the Corinthians were rediscovered and published at Oxford in 1633 and whose "venerable autority" Milton cites in *The Reason of Church Government Urged Against Prelaty*,[33] was the

---

two of the sects as follows (*op. cit.,* VI, 683): "As in his middle life the Baptists and other very free varieties of Independents had been most to his taste, so in his later years he seems to have found much to like in the religious habits of the Quakers."

[29] *Of Prelatical Episcopacy,* Columbia Edition, III, 86.
[30] *Eikonoklastes,* Columbia Edition, V, 206.
[31] *Of True Religion, Heresy, Schism,* Columbia Edition, VI, 174.
[32] *The Christian Doctrine,* Columbia Edition, XIV, 61.
[33] Columbia Edition, III, 211.

first to raise the question of sinlessness as a necessary characteristic
of Christian perfection.[34] It was his belief that sinlessness in this
life, and therefore perfection, were possible and were expected of
adherents of the Christian Church. Similarly Hermas, Justin Martyr,
Irenaeus, and others whom Milton refers to in his prose tracts declared that those who know and love God are freed from sin. In
the words of Irenaeus: "Those, then, are the perfect who have had
the Spirit of God remaining in them." [35] To Clement of Alexandria,
also, regeneration meant sinlessness and therefore perfection: "Being
baptized, we are illuminated; illuminated, we become sons; being
made sons, we are made perfect; being made perfect, we are made
immortal." [36] Though Paul had taught that perfection is to be attained by "overcoming" the world—that is, passing through it,
taking it in, thereby understanding it and going beyond—to Origen,
precursor of monasticism, "the perfect Christian is one who at the
summit of his progress has turned his back on the outward and
visible world as well as on the emotions of mankind," [37] lest his
senses lead him astray; and thus began monasticism, "the boldest
organized attempt to attain to Christian perfection in all the long
history of the Church." [38] Christ's charge to the Rich Young Ruler
to sell all and give to the poor "if thou wouldst be perfect" provided
the immediate motivation of St. Anthony, St. Basil, St. Benedict,
and other founders of monasticism, though their vows of poverty,
celibacy, and removal from the world made their path to perfection
possible only to the few. Later the possibility of perfection was
approved by Franciscans, Jesuits, Molinists, but denied by Domini-
cans and Jansenists.[39]

Augustine's perfectionism was based on love, rather than sinlessness, for to him only Christ and his Mother, among mortals, were
without sin.[40] This love for God and man, if perfect, would produce
such delight as to overcome every opposite tendency. The "excellentia Dei," which Augustine defined as "aliquid quo nihil melius

[34] Cf. Flew, *op. cit.*, pp. 131–32.      [35] Quoted in *ibid.*, p. 137.
[36] *Ibid.*, p. 148.      [37] *Ibid.*, p. 151.
[38] *Ibid.*, p. 158.      [39] Platt, "Perfection," *loc. cit.*, p. 733.
[40] Cf. Flew, *op. cit.*, pp. 193–216; also Platt, "Perfection," *loc. cit.*, p. 733.

est," [41] was his Summum Bonum, a good which is attainable by man, through love, here on earth "in the measure of human perfection in which perfection is possible in this life," [42] but which reaches its fullness beyond the grave. The three degrees of perfection possible in this life, according to St. Augustine, were those of the beginners, the proficients, and the perfect—a classification corresponding to the purgative, illuminative, and unitive categories of Dionysius.[43] Augustine's emphasis on love as the basis of perfection has remained the core of Christian doctrine ever since; but his idea of the Summum Bonum, like that of Greek philosophy, again imposes the concept of an end to the perfection of both God and man, an end limited by the human intellect and therefore intolerable. Also his belief in the achievement of perfection by stages is a recurrence of the static idea of ultimate completion and not of the "excellentia" which implies "dynamic movement beyond a limit." [44]

"Of all theologians," says R. Newton Flew, "St. Thomas is the most dominated by the thought of the ultimate perfection of mankind." [45] To him man's very nature implied a goal in goodness, and like Augustine, he believed that Christian perfection is achieved through love,[46] which unites man with God, the highest good. In reply to the question of whether perfection may be achieved in this life, he indicated what to him was the three-fold nature of perfection: [47] first was the absolute perfection of God, a totality from which nothing is lacking; second was complete love of man for God, not to be achieved in this life, since here we are only on the way to the perfection of heaven; third was man's removal, from his habits and affections, of every obstacle to love of God, a perfection possible in this life. In both his *Summa Theologica* and his *De Perfectione,* he praises monastic vows and religious orders as the surest and shortest way to perfection. He introduces the idea of

[41] *De Doctrina Christiana,* I, 7. Quoted by Foss, *op. cit.,* p. 31, n. 18.
[42] *Retractions,* I, 19. Quoted by Flew, *op. cit.,* p. 208.
[43] Cf. Garrigou-Lagrange, *op. cit.,* p. 5. A table, p. 6, shows the progress of this doctrine from St. Augustine to St. Theresa.
[44] Cf. Foss, *op. cit.,* pp. 31–33.      [45] Flew, *op. cit.,* p. 225.
[46] *Ibid.,* pp. 234 ff. Cf. also Garrigou-Lagrange, *op. cit.,* pp. 135–39.
[47] Flew, *op. cit.,* pp. 236 ff.

relative merit for relative degrees of perfection. Bishops are in a state of perfection, he says, because in their office they confer grace and enlightenment on others. Religious orders are second in merit because they are being perfected. Parish priests and archdeacons are third in this hierarchy of perfection, and all others are below them, as capable of attainment of the third kind of perfection. St. Thomas' emphasis on the advantages of religious office or of monastic vows in the quest for perfection was later a point of attack by the Reformers, to whom all men, regardless of vocation, were equally capable of and equally committed to the quest for Christian perfection. In his use of the method of analogy between finite and infinite, moreover, Aquinas "reduces the infinity of God to a finitude, restores the old Greek limitation, and is the cause of a revival of the fallacy of divine perfection in most of the great systems of modern philosophy. It is the rationalization and mechanization of religious thought throughout the Renaissance which Aquinas' method of analogy brought into existence." [48] The Aristotelian idea of finite perfection, as one part of total or infinite perfection, was restored, and with it all the limitations of an end desired rather than a way of life to be followed.

It remained for Duns Scotus and his followers to remove these limitations of the idea of perfection.[49] He conceived of the "absolute and unique individual," by whom the unique and absolute God may be approached through intuition, so that the divine in man makes it possible for him to know the divine in God and to identify himself with God. In this concept of individuality, the Thomist idea of mere quantitative difference and hence of totality and limitation is no longer conceivable. Moreover, with Duns Scotus came the new and dynamic concept of Infinity, unlike the Greek idea of infinity as chaos, and with him came also the new Christian doctrine of perfection as excellence, a surmounting of barriers. This new concept of perfection implied a way of life rather than completion of goodness as an end. For the attainment of these concepts, the Greek belief in identifying intuition and Augustine's stress on the

---

[48] Foss, *op. cit.*, p. 42.          [49] *Ibid.*, pp. 37 ff.

necessity of constant seeking for truth provided a foundation, but it was the Franciscan philosopher Duns Scotus and his followers who saw the implications of such ideas for Christian doctrine.

The word *Perfektionismus* was used by the theologians of the Reformation chiefly in disapproval of monasticism and of the new sect of Anabaptists, whose creed included belief in sinlessness and therefore perfection in this life.[50] Such doctrine the Augsburg Confession strongly condemned. Sin in this life, said Luther, is inevitable; perfection, therefore, may be striven for but not attained except in the hereafter. Calvin, also, stressing Augustine's limitations of perfection in this life rather than the Biblical adjurations to perfection, regarded this life as only a progress toward perfection, a goal not to be attained "until we have laid aside the body of sin and been completely united to the Lord."[51] Similarly the Reformers denounced the perfectionism of monasticism. "It doth not consist in celibacy, or mendicancy, or in vile apparel," says the Augsburg Confession. Rather it is "to fear God sincerely, and again to conceive great faith, and to trust that for Christ's sake God is pacified toward us; to ask, and with certainty to look for, help from God in all our affairs, according to our calling; and meantime outwardly to do good works diligently and to attend to our calling."[52] The use of the term *perfection* was limited by the Reformers to the idea of perfection by imputation. Christ's goodness, in the human state, was a kind of justification for all mankind; and the Christian's only hope of perfection in this life was of excellence completed in Christ and imputed to man by God through His grace.[53] Such imputation of righteousness implies, however, that moral character is transferable—a position later ardently attacked. Melancthon, in his *Apologia,* came closest, among the Reformers, to a belief in man's own perfection, for he did not dismiss the fact that the Bible commands perfection; and in his vision of a better and better world, achieved through the humanism of the ancients as well as through

[50] Cf. Flew, *op. cit.,* pp. 244–57.
[51] *Institutes,* Book II, 412. Quoted by Flew, *op. cit.,* p. 244.
[52] Augsburg Confession. Quoted by Flew, *op. cit.,* p. 246.
[53] Cf. Platt, *loc. cit.,* p. 732.

Christianity, he assumed the perfectibility of mankind, though he did not call it by that name. Lutheranism did not flourish as might have been expected; and some have ascribed its subsequent decline to its lack of a positive doctrine of perfection.[54] As John Wesley said later, "The work of God does not prosper where perfect love is not preached." [55] To those Anglicans who later became Methodists, as well as to the Pietists, Baptists, and Quakers before them, the necessity of aiming at perfection was obvious.

Between the Reformers of the sixteenth century and Milton and the sects in the seventeenth century stand Arminius (1560–1609) and the Cambridge Platonists. The theology of freedom and toleration of the Dutch scholar Jacobus Hermans, or Arminius, which greatly influenced the teaching of the Cambridge divines,[56] prepared the way for resistance against the absolutism of Calvin by the numerous sects that arose in western Europe and especially in England in the seventeenth and eighteenth centuries. Arminianism was the form of Reformation theology that best suited and most strengthened the humanism of the Renaissance and the scientific advance of the seventeenth century at the same time that it taught man's need of God, who was to be found through knowledge and reason. Unlike Lutheranism, Arminianism supplied man with a goal, namely, Christian perfection. The Reformation had brought the ideal of perfection out into the open, and to Arminius perfection was attainable in this life. It was to be attained by degrees like those of Augustine and Thomas Aquinas: beginners, proficients, the truly perfect.[57] In the words of Episcopius, follower of Arminius: "It is not sinless or an absolutely perfect obedience, but such as consists in a sincere love of piety, absolutely excluding every habit of sin." [58] The writings of the Arminian scholars, especially Episcopius, were much read by the Cambridge Platonists,[59] and in

[54] *Ibid.*, p. 254.        [55] Quoted by Flew, *op. cit.*, Intro., p. xiii.

[56] Frederic Platt, "Arminianism," *Encyclopedia of Religion and Ethics*, I, 813.

[57] Platt, "Perfection," *loc. cit.*, IX, 732.

[58] *Ibid.* Quoted from *Institutiones Theologiae Christianae* (Amsterdam, 1715), pp. 658a, 659b.

[59] Cf. J. A. Stewart, "Cambridge Platonists," *Encyclopedia of Religion and Ethics*, III, 167–73.

their teachings of toleration, of the universality and reasonableness of religion, of the importance of knowledge, both ancient and Christian, in man's quest for God, as well as in their belief in each man's right and ability, through reason, to interpret the Scriptures, they, too, helped prepare the way for the sects at the same time that they maintained the unity between humanism and Christianity so characteristic of Milton. They helped to prepare the way for Milton's eloquent plea in the *Areopagitica* for tolerance for the sects, on the one hand, and for prudence and forbearance and charity that would permit all men "to joyn and unite into one generall and brotherly search after Truth," [60] on the other. Henry More was especially interested in *theologica Germanica,* and it was he who described how man, in his search for God, becomes more and more like God, until the perfection of reason is reached in God's "Divine sagacity." [61] Reason, as the chief means to religion, made Natural and Revealed Religion alike to the Cambridge divines. Plato was their *"Moses Atticus."* [62] The ecstasy of union with God described by Plato and Plotinus was to them similar to that of the man "in whom Christ liveth." Thus they reunited Christianity and Platonic philosophy, though not in the manner of Thomas Aquinas or Descartes, for in their efforts to divert the philosophy of Descartes and Hobbes from materialism and atheism to the defense of religion and a spiritual interpretation of the world, they conceived the theory of the "plastic principle" or "soul of nature," somewhat like Plato's *anima mundi,* which is infinite in scope and which is the first and ever-present cause of all things. The teleology of the Cambridge Platonists thus inferred Infinite Spirit, whose Divine wisdom and goodness were conceivable and attainable by the immortal soul through the operation of the "plastic principle" [63] and through the use of reason and knowledge. The Cambridge theologians were almost the only teachers of the early seventeenth century who taught

---

[60] Columbia Edition, IV, 341.

[61] Stewart, "Cambridge Platonists," *loc. cit.,* p. 168. Quoted from the Preface to *A Collection of Several Philosophical Writings of Dr. H. More* (London: W. Morden, 1662), p. ix.                    [62] *Ibid.*

[63] *Ibid.,* p. 170. Cf. Ralph Cudworth, *The True Intellectual System of the Universe* (ed. 1845), I, 274 ff.

that man's achievement of Christian perfection required the use
of his own reason and experience [64]—a belief that was indispensable
to the sects and was to be the chief tenet of Milton's philosophy.

Milton's indebtedness to the Cambridge Platonists, though he
never mentions them, is obvious.[65] The influence of the Cambridge
Platonists on some of the sectaries, especially the Quakers, is less
common knowledge and may profitably be noted. Henry More was
spiritual adviser of Lady Conway, of Ragley in Worcestershire,
who became a Quaker. He was also a friend of Descartes and of
the Stuart Princess Elizabeth, Princess Palatine of the Rhine, one
of the most learned women in Europe, who, in her later years, was
almost persuaded to become a Quaker. Her distant cousin and
adviser was Robert Barclay of Scotland, a well-trained scholar, who
formulated the Quaker faith of George Fox and others into a system
of theology. Barclay, however, had not read "the fresh and liberating
interpretations of Christianity given by the Cambridge Platonists,
Benjamin Whichcote, John Smith, and their friends . . . a way of
thought kindred to the spirit and genius of the Quaker principle
and ideals," [66] so that Quakerism declined after his time. John
Norris, rector of Bemerton, who was influenced by the Cambridge
Platonists, especially Henry More, was able to show the inadequacy
of Barclay's interpretation of Quaker doctrine.[67] That the sectaries
were by no means all ignorant, uneducated enthusiasts is, of course,
evident from the reading of the histories of the foundings of the
new faiths.[68] Such men and women of station and education as
William Penn and Isaac Penington of Buckinghamshire, a Quaker
center not far from Horton, where, in Chalfont St. Giles, Thomas
Ellwood sequestered Milton during the time of plague; Lady Clay-
pool, daughter of Cromwell, who was a Seeker; Roger Williams,

[64] Stewart, "Cambridge Platonists," *loc. cit.,* p. 172.
[65] Cf. Hanford, *op. cit.,* pp. 235–36, 246, 362.
[66] William C. Braithwaite, *The Second Period of Quakerism* (London: Macmillan Company, 1919), Intro. by Rufus M. Jones, p. xxxiii.
[67] *Ibid.,* p. 392.
[68] Cf. also Wolfe, *op. cit.,* pp. 28, 70–77, and Louise Fargo Brown, *The Political Activities of the Baptists and Fifth Monarchy Men in England during the Interregnum* (New York: Oxford University Press, 1912), pp. 9–11.

first Baptist, then Seeker; Henry Lawrence, president of the Council of State of the Protectorate, "most eminent Baptist in the eyes of men of that generation"; [69] William Steele, Recorder of London, Baptist; Vice Admiral Lawson of the Fleet, Baptist; such Baptist scholars as John Tombes, Oxford theologian, and Willian Dell, master of Caius College, Cambridge; Hanserd Knollys, Benjamin Cox, Francis Cornwall, Baptist printers and financiers; and, in the Army, the Baptist Colonels, Robert Bennet, Richard Overton, Charles Howard, Robert Lilburne, John Hutchinson, Richard Deane, Henry Danvers, John Wigan; as well as others of lesser rank, such as John Bunyan, a "vehement Baptist," and John Lilburne, who became a Baptist on October 4, 1645—all these prove that, like Lollardry, the truth of the sects appealed to people of reason and insight, regardless of rank. The fact that in the beginning the sects thought of themselves as societies or communities of believers who had been reborn, rather than as churches,[70] made it possible for adherents to accept their faith while still Anglican or, as in the case of Milton, to hold ideas similar to theirs without being a member of any church or sect.

The significance of Quakerism in the history of the idea of perfection and the great similarity between Quaker doctrine and Milton's beliefs have been fully treated by R. Newton Flew in his *Idea of Perfection in Christian Theology* [71] and by Alden Sampson in his *Studies in Milton,*[72] respectively. What is less commonly known and recognized is that Quakerism was an outgrowth of the Baptist movement and that most of the doctrines and church organization of the Quakers were derived directly from those of the Baptists.[73]

[69] Brown, *op. cit.,* p. 9.

[70] Cf. Max Weber, *The Protestant Ethic and the Spirit of Capitalism* (New York: Charles Scribner's Sons, 1930), pp. 144–45. See also *Of True Religion, Heresy, Schism,* Columbia Edition, VI, 167–68, where Milton defines *sect* and *schism.*

[71] Pages 281–92.                  [72] Pages 167 ff.

[73] Cf. William C. Braithwaite, *Beginnings of Quakerism* (London: Macmillan Company, 1912), pp. 12, 43–45, 142; also Robert Barclay, *The Inner Life of the Religious Societies of the Commonwealth* (3d ed.; London: Hodder and Stoughton, 1879), pp. 10 ff.; also Weber, *op. cit.,* p. 252 n. 169 and p. 256 n. 181; William Tallack, *George Fox, the Friends, and the Early Baptists* (London: S. W. Partridge, 1868), pp. 65 ff.; and Flew, *op. cit.,* p. 284.

Being Arminian in faith and therefore opposed to the Calvinistic doctrines of original sin and predestination, the Baptist movement and the sects derived from it in the course of the sixteenth and seventeenth centuries, especially the Baptists, Mennonites, and Quakers,[74] based their faith on the perfectibility of all men through an "Inner Light," a continual revelation of truth by the Holy Spirit, whereby man might attain to real, not imputed holiness. To them, reason and knowledge were not enough; nor were the Scriptures their sole authority. To achieve holiness, the Christian must open his heart to the Spirit, wait quietly for it to descend, and through its power conquer sin. Then, by stages of development and with the help of the new understanding of the Scriptures made possible by this "Inner Light," he might reach a state of perfection in this life like that of Adam and Eve before the Fall. Such a faith required freedom of worship. Consequently, the Baptists also stood for: complete separation of church and state; wide religious toleration; baptism only of adults, who had attained their own faith; baptism by immersion, since Christ was so baptized; simplicity of life and worship, as in the primitive or apostolic community; independence of each community of believers; itinerant lay preachers and elders, as described in the New Testament; opposition to tithes and a "hireling ministry." Most of these Baptist tenets, in the ministry of George Fox, became the tenets of Quakerism; and all of them were tenets held by Milton and variously expressed in the prose tracts and the *De Doctrina Christiana,* even to a defense of immersion [75] and immersion for adults only.[76] Such purely Quaker tenets as refusal to take oaths or carry arms or hold public office did not

[74] Weber, *op. cit.,* p. 144.

[75] *The Christian Doctrine,* Columbia Edition, XVI, 183.

[76] *Ibid.,* pp. 171, 183. Milton would not, however, have approved of Baptist acceptance of women preachers. Cf. *ibid.,* p. 327, where he cites Scripture to prove that "Women . . . are enjoined to keep silence in the church." Milton's statement concerning the power of the Spirit, in *ibid.,* pp. 273–75: "Under the gospel we possess . . . a twofold Scripture, one external, which is the written word, and the other internal, which is the Holy Spirit, written in the hearts of believers. . . . That which is internal . . . is far superior to all," is, according to William Ellery Channing, *Works,* I, 57, "genuine Quakerism." Milton's unitarianism, however, had it been fully realized at the time, would have barred him from both the Baptist and the Quaker sects.

meet with Milton's approval.[77] Quaker abandonment of baptism and communion, however, he would have condoned, inasmuch as "sacraments are not absolutely indispensable." [78] In his later defense of the sects, Milton mentions the "Anabaptists," along with the Lutherans, Calvinists, Arians, Socinians, and Arminians, though he does not mention the Quakers or Friends.[79]

The first English Baptist Church, formed of refugee Independents and Separatists in Amsterdam under the leadership of John Smyth and Thomas Helwys, in 1611 published their declaration of faith. They asserted their objection to infant baptism and their conviction that "the magistrate is not by vertue of his office to meddle with religion, or matters of conscience, to force and compell men to this or that form of doctrine." This declaration is "the first known expression of absolute liberty of conscience in any confession of faith." [80] In 1612, after the death of Smyth, Helwys returned with his church to London. There they were called General Baptists (Arminian) as distinguished from a group formed later called Particular Baptists because of their Calvinistic leanings. The sect grew in numbers, teaching their doctrines in the midst of persecution until the Toleration Act of 1689. Henry Denne, the greatest preacher among the General Baptists and one of a score of Anglican clergy who were becoming Baptists and ardent propagandists,[81] explained the Baptist doctrine of Inner Light in his book *The Dragnet,* published in 1646.[82] The following year George Fox, whose uncle Pickering was a Baptist, joined a "shattered" (that is, divided) Baptist Society at Mansfield in Nottinghamshire and there found fellowship and peace in the Baptist doctrines. Under his leadership the two groups reunited, calling themselves "Children of the Light," and later became the first Quaker congregation. Thus Fox became the founder of a new sect or society. In the course of time he won

[77] *The Christian Doctrine,* Columbia Edition, XVII, 119 ff. and 385 ff.

[78] *Ibid.,* XVI, 201.

[79] *Of True Religion, Heresy, Schism,* Columbia Edition, VI, 169.

[80] *Encyclopedia Britannica* (1947 ed.), III, 87.

[81] William Thomas Whitley, *A History of British Baptists* (London: Charles Griffin and Company, 1923), p. 70.

[82] Braithwaite, *Beginnings of Quakerism,* p. 12.

many Baptist converts to Quakerism, thereby rousing the resistance and resentment of the other Baptists.[83]

Quaker doctrine was powerful, precisely because of its teaching of perfection.[84] Fox rejected the prevailing Calvinistic concentration on sin, and turned instead to a faith in man's holiness. Having experienced the Inner Light and having carefully studied the Bible, he was convinced that the doctrine of Inner Light must mean freedom from sin; and the holiness he taught was not imputed but real. Such perfection, moreover, was attainable in this life. Living in an age when the church was thought to be pitted against a world lost in sin, when the natural life of man was carnal and a prey to evil until salvation was visited upon him by the grace of God, Fox no doubt shared the teachings of his time. In 1648, however, at the age of twenty-four, he experienced the "miracle of illumination," which became the Quaker message. No more remarkable expression of this new faith in man's perfectibility can be found than that in Fox's *Journal,* I, 56. The statement is the more remarkable in the light of Milton's faith as set forth in *Paradise Lost.* Fox wrote:

> Now I was come up in spirit through the flaming sword, into the paradise of God. All things were new; and all creation gave another smell unto me than before, beyond what words can utter. I knew nothing but pureness, and innocency, and righteousness, being renewed up into the image of God by Christ Jesus, to the state of Adam, which he was in before he fell. . . . But I was immediately taken up in spirit to see into another or more steadfast state than Adam's in innocency, even into a state in Christ Jesus that should never fall. And the Lord shewed me that such as were faithful to Him, in the power and light of Christ, should come up into that state in which Adam was before he fell; in which the admirable works of the creation, and the virtues thereof, may be known through the openings of that divine Word of wisdom and power by which they were made.[85]

---

[83] *Ibid.,* pp. 142, 170, 396.     [84] Cf. Flew, *op. cit.,* pp. 282 ff.
[85] *Journal* (London: J. M. Dent and Sons, 1924), p. 17. Quoted by Flew, *op. cit.,* p. 286.

Here, in little, is the conclusion of *Paradise Lost*. Fox, like Adam
through the "Fortunate Fall," found a state of wisdom and goodness
even "more steadfast" than that of Adam and Eve in Paradise. Like
Adam, he also learned to know "the admirable works of the creation
and the virtues thereof." And in his later teachings, like Adam
again, Fox saw all the world before him, a place where a perfection
of undying love and service was demanded, even unto suffering.
Such was Fox's interpretation of the meaning of the Cross or the
Atonement. The Atonement, he said, was inward; it was suffering
"that crucifies you to the state that Adam and Eve were in, in the
Fall." [86] Fox's emphasis on love and service and suffering is Milton's
conclusion as well:

> Henceforth I learne, that to obey is best,
> And love with feare the onely God, to walk
> As in his presence, ever to observe
> His providence, and on him sole depend,
> Merciful over all his works, with good
> Still overcoming evil, and by small
> Accomplishing great things, by things deemed weak
> Subverting worldly strong, and worldly wise
> By simply meek; that suffering for Truths sake
> Is fortitude to highest victorie.[87]

Such perfection is that of humility. In it there is none of the unbearable pride of "the ethical perfectionist, the virtuoso of virtue,
the man without defects, self-sure and proud of himself." [88] Moreover, it is the perfection of activity, quite unlike that of Dante
in Paradise. The end of *The Divine Comedy* brings the soul to a
state of perfection, or completion, in contemplation. There the soul
is "laid to rest and despoiled of its own powers." [89] Luther and the
Reformers had made that concept of perfection no longer tenable;
and so Fox, like Milton, saw perfection in love as a source of service;

[86] Quoted by Flew, *op. cit.*, p. 291, from Fox's *Journal*, I, 345.
[87] *Paradise Lost*, Book XII, ll. 561-70.        [88] Cf. Foss, *op. cit.*, p. 86.
[89] Flew, *op. cit.*, p. 253. Cf. also Weber, *op. cit.*, pp. 87-88.

love that "sees always beyond, is always on the way to more and better"; [90] love that accepts sacrifice and suffering, if need be. In the words of Michael at the close of *Paradise Lost:*

> Onely add
> Deeds to thy knowledge answerable, add Faith,
> Add Vertue, Patience, Temperance, add Love,
> By name to come call'd Charitie, the soul
> Of all the rest; then wilt thou not be loath
> To leave this Paradise, but shalt possess
> A Paradise within thee, happier farr. [91]

Persecution of the Quakers was mainly due to their refusal to take oaths, pay tithes, and bear arms, but they were also attacked and derided for their belief in human perfection. [92] When they were accused of boasting of perfection, they replied, "We *own* perfection, but we do *not* boast of it!" They explained it as "a going on unto perfection" and as a perfection in the measure that was attainable. "Would Christ and His Apostles," they asked, "constantly urge this going on unto perfection, if a state answering to their intentions were unattainable?" [93] While in prison in Derby in 1650, Fox assured those who came to him pleading sin and imperfection that they might be freed from sin in this life if they would wait for the Spirit and purify their hearts. [94]

Nevertheless, Fox's disciples sought to protect their faith from the charge of fanaticism. William Penn, in *A Testimony to the Truth of God,* [95] concluded his explanation of the Quaker doctrine of sinlessness with a reservation:

Because we have urged the necessity of a perfect freedom from sin, and a thorough sanctification in body, soul, and spirit, whilst on this side the grave, by the operation of the holy and perfect Spirit of our Lord Jesus Christ, according to the testimony of

[90] Foss, *op. cit.,* p. 86.
[91] *Paradise Lost,* Book XII, ll. 581–87.
[92] Cf. Barclay, *op. cit.,* p. 337.
[93] *Ibid.,* p. 337 n. 3.
[94] Flew, *op. cit.,* p. 285; *Journal,* II, 30–39.
[95] *Select Works* (3d ed.; London: James Phillips, 1782), V, 342. Quoted by Flew, *op. cit.,* p. 287.

the holy scripture, we are made [that is, represented as being] so presumptuous, as to assert the fulness of perfection and happiness to be attainable in this life: whereas we are not only sensible of those human infirmities that attend us, whilst clothed with flesh and blood; but know that here we can only "know in part, and see in part": the perfection of wisdom, glory, and happiness, being reserved for another and better world.

Similarly, Robert Barclay, who formulated Quaker doctrine in a Lutheran and Calvinistic fashion, asserted the incompleteness of perfection in this life. Those who have found the Inner Light may, he said, be "free from actual sinning and transgressing the law of God, and in that respect perfect: yet doth this perfection still admit of a growth, and there remaineth always in some part a possibility of sinning." [96] But Barclay, well versed in the writings of the Church Fathers, the Schoolmen, and the Reformers, though ignorant of the teachings of Arminius and the Cambridge Platonists, returned to the doctrine of total depravity and sought to "lock up this new idea [of the Inner Light] in that old system" of Reformation theology.[97] To Barclay, man was "miserable," "depraved," "unspiritual," "without capacity for salvation" except by the grace of God. After Barclay's time, Quakerism languished, though the spirit of Fox's faith in humankind never died. Such works as William Law's *Treatise of Christian Perfection* (1726) and John Wesley's *Plain Account of Christian Perfection* (1725) proved the persistence of the ideal and a continued faith in its realization. To Matthew Arnold culture became "the study of perfection," and to Bentham and his followers perfection became a utility, necessary to society and possible for all. The utilitarians, however, again reduced the concept to an end, rather than a way, and thus deprived it of its ethical value. It was against this ethics of ends that Kant inveighed until he "broke the power of this concept at its core." [98]

In 1643 and 1644, while the sect of Baptists was spreading in

[96] Cf. Flew, *op. cit.*, p. 288.
[97] Cf. Braithwaite, *Second Period of Quakerism*, Intro. by Rufus M. Jones, p. xxxiii.
[98] Foss, *op. cit.*, p. 76.

England and before George Fox's ministry had begun, Milton's growing anti-Presbyterianism culminated in his strong defense of the sects in the *Areopagitica* and in *On the New Forcers of Conscience*. In at least ten places in the *Areopagitica*[99] he voices his belief in sects and schisms as sources of truth. The Christian faith itself was once a schism, he says. Wycliff, "the divine and admirable spirit," was a schismatic; and had it not been for the attempts to suppress him, Huss, Jerome, Luther, and Calvin might never have been heard of. The sects and schisms, so bitterly complained of, only prove how live is faith in England. How Moses must rejoice in heaven to see that "not only our seventy elders, but all the Lord's people, are become prophets!" London has become a "city of refuge, the mansion-house of liberty," in its ardent quest for truth. "A gross conforming stupidity" is far more dangerous than "many sub-dichotomies of petty schisms." Suppression of sects only increases their zeal. And who is there who does not profit from their inquiries? Speaking plainly for himself, Milton advises "liberal and frequent audience" for schismatics, even though they be erroneous, "seeing no man who hath tasted learning, but will confess the many ways of profiting by those who, not contented with stale receipts, are able to manage and set forth new positions to the world." Reading such a plea for tolerance, one finds it easy to believe that Milton himself did not close his ears to the teachings of the sects and that his own Christian doctrine, though independent of any one sect or creed, was influenced in part by the teachings of many of them. In *On the New Forcers of Conscience* Milton again voiced the views of the early Independents, Baptists, Quakers, and thousands of other sectaries concerning the intolerance of the Presbyterian Parliament and the Westminster Assembly of Divines. His defense of the sects and of their views continued in *Means to Remove Hirelings out of the Church, Of True Religion, Heresy, Schism*, and *The Christian Doctrine*, and Cromwell's toleration of all faiths inspired Milton's plea to him to "save free Conscience from the paw of hireling wolves."

[99] Columbia Edition, IV, 321, 332–33, 339, 341, 342, 343, 346, 349, 351–52.

Nor was Milton unacquainted with the sectaries themselves. Roger Williams, who, according to Masson, went to see Milton on his visits to England, was a Baptist and later a Seeker. In 1663 Milton married Elizabeth Minshull, a Baptist,[100] niece of the eminent London physician, Dr. Nathan Paget; Milton called her his "very kind wife."[101] Henry Vane, Henry Lawrence, and others whom Milton met in public life were Independents or avowed members of the other sects. In 1662 Dr. Paget introduced Thomas Ellwood, Quaker, to Milton; and Ellwood served as Milton's reader, though "not as a servant," as he himself says,[102] and remained Milton's friend until Milton's death.

Some of the misstatements concerning Ellwood and the apparent lack of information as to his life and station and character make desirable a reconsideration of his background and his relations with Milton. Mark Pattison's statement that Ellwood was "the reverse of humble"[103] and Masson's epithet of a "somewhat thick-headed" man who "grew up a rough country lad fond of nothing but horses, dogs, and field sports"[104] until the age of twenty have slight basis in fact, for his autobiography and the testimonies of his friends printed with it give exactly the opposite impression. Joseph Wyeth, who edited Ellwood's *History* of himself, characterized Ellwood as follows: "A man of a comely aspect, of a free and generous disposition, of a courteous and affable temper, and pleasant conversation; a gentleman born and bred, a scholar, a true Christian, an eminent author, a good neighbour, and a kind friend."[105] Socially Ellwood ranked above Milton and was therefore not a typical representative of the Quaker movement.[106] Son and later the heir of

[100] Masson, *op. cit.*, VI, 745, 747.     [101] *Ibid.*, VI, 728.
[102] *The History of Thomas Ellwood Written by Himself* (London: George Routledge and Sons, 1885), p. 133.
[103] *Milton* (London: Macmillan Company, 1900), p. 149.
[104] Masson, *op. cit.*, VI, 496 and 467.
[105] Cf. Alfred Kemp Brown, "Thomas Ellwood, the Friend of Milton," *Friends Ancient and Modern*, No. 15 (London: Headley Brothers, 1910), p. 36.
[106] Cf. Beatrice Saxon Snell, "The Making of Thomas Ellwood," *Journal of the Friends' Historical Society*, XXXVI (1939), 21–47; also Arthur Rowntree, "Thomas Ellwood," *Friends' Quarterly Examiner*, LXXIII (July and October, 1939), 248–60, 295–308.

a country gentleman, who possessed "a pretty estate in lands and
more as I have heard in moneys," [107] he was related on his mother's
side to the great Puritan family of Hampdens. While his older
brother went to Oxford, Thomas, who also had "a genius apt to
learn," remained on his father's estate, "to retrench expenses." [108]
Because of his dislike of "scurrilities in conversation" and of "im-
moderate drinking," he was "acceptable to persons of the best note"
and often visited at Thame Park, the home of Lord Wenman, who
"had been pleased to bestow his name upon me, when he made
large promises for me at the font" and whose lady, formerly
Margaret Hampden, was closely related to Ellwood's mother.[109]
Lord Wenman would probably have fulfilled his large promises if
Ellwood had not been, in his own words, "called into the service
of the best and highest Lord, and thereby lost the favour of all my
friends, relations, and acquaintances of this world." In Civil War
times, during Thomas' childhood, the Ellwoods remained in London,
where they became the close friends of Lady Springett; she later
became Mrs. Isaac Penington, Quaker, and her daughter Gulielma,
though wooed by Ellwood, later became Mrs. William Penn. Ellwood's friendship with the Peningtons led to his service for seven
years as tutor in their home in Buckinghamshire.

Ellwood made up for the loss of formal education by reading,
a habit that he returned to after his conversion to Quakerism. Feeling keenly the injustice of the charge that Quakers "despised and
decried all human learning," Ellwood applied himself "with utmost
diligence, and at all leisure times," to study.[110] Though suffering
an attack of smallpox in 1661, on his recovery he began to read
again in his father's library. His description of the library as a
"pretty good" one, "amongst which were the works of Augustine
and others of those ancient writers who were by many called the
fathers," makes one realize the extent of his reading. The fact that
the books were "printed in the old black letter, with abbreviations
of the words difficult to be read," meant that Ellwood "spent too

107 Ellwood, *op. cit.*, p. 10.     108 *Ibid.*, p. 13.
109 *Ibid.*, p. 15.     110 *Ibid.*, p. 131.

much time therein, and thereby much impaired my sight, which was not strong before, and was now weaker than usual by reason of the illness I had so newly had, which proved an injury to me afterwards." [111] Nevertheless, his desire to learn led to a complaint about his difficulties to Isaac Penington, who, through Dr. Paget, introduced him to Milton, and for Milton he read until another illness and imprisonment prevented further visits. It was Ellwood, however, who found Milton a refuge in Chalfont St. Giles, near his own home in Chalfont St. Peters; who read *Paradise Lost* in manuscript; and who made his well-known suggestion of a *Paradise Regained*. Altogether Milton and Ellwood apparently had much more in common than is ordinarily supposed. He seems to have been a man of sterling worth, who "modestly accepted the career that opened before him, and filled its limited opportunities with countless kindly offices and unwearied literary work." [112] His *Life* is full of charm, and his editing of Fox's *Journal* in 1694 is "the most important literary event in the history of the Friends." [113]

No less interesting is the life of Isaac Penington, "son of a Parliament Grandee," who had been reared in Puritan surroundings of refinement.[114] In 1658, at the mature age of forty-two, he joined the despised Quakers. Of the remaining twenty-one years of his life he spent five in prison, often in such cold, damp rooms that his life was endangered. Of him one of the Buckinghamshire Friends said: "I do not remember that ever I saw him cast down or dejected in his spirit in the time of his close confinement, nor speak hardly of those that persecuted him." [115] His assertion that in Quakerism he had "met with the true Peace, the true Righteousness, the true Holiness, the true rest of Soul, the everlasting habitation which the redeemed dwell in" [116] supplies reason for his endurance as well as proof of the efficacy of the Quaker ideal of perfection. Masson's assertion that "as in his Milton's middle life the Baptists and other

---

[111] *Ibid.*      [112] Braithwaite, *The Second Period of Quakerism*, pp. 422 ff.
[113] *Ibid.*, p. 427.      [114] *Ibid.*, p. 381.      [115] *Ibid.*
[116] *The Works of the Long-Mournful and Sorely-Distressed Isaac Penington* (London: Benjamin Clark, 1681), on the 6th page of "The Testimony of Thomas Ellwood concerning Isaac Penington." Quoted by Flew, *op. cit.*, p. 283.

very free varieties of Independents had been most to his taste, so in his later years he seems to have found much to like in the religious habits of the Quakers" may be due in no small measure to the loyalty of such Friends as he knew in times of his greatest danger and need. They were the times when, "though fall'n on evil dayes . . . and evil tongues; in darkness, and with dangers compast round, and solitude," he, too, knew the power of a sustaining inner light and wrote his greatest works. Like Penington, he voiced no complaints about his sad state, buoyed up by the "Celestial Song" of Urania, "by that name if rightly thou art call'd."

It remains to determine more exactly what Milton's conclusions were concerning the problem of human perfection. Cognizant of the doctrines of those about him and before him, he was obliged to choose among them or to reject them and formulate his own. Since his chief authority was the Bible, his conclusions are carefully weighed decisions, based on his own interpretation of Old and New Testament passages. To that interpretation he brought such learning, such wisdom and insight, such passion for moral excellence as few interpreters have provided.

Milton's concern with the problem of perfection, as might be expected, begins with the prose works. In the Minor Poems his use of the word *perfect* is simply that of "full" or "complete." The "full and perfect bliss" of the *Nativity Hymn,* the "perfet tumult of loud Mirth" in *Comus,* the "perfect misery" of the unwary victim of Comus, the "perfet witness of all judging Jove" in *Lycidas,* and the tears of "perfect moan" shed for the Marchioness of Winchester all imply completion, with much the same meaning as Isaac Walton expressed in discussing "the compleat angler" or Henry Peacham in describing "the compleat gentleman." Prosody could approve *perfet* where *compleat* would not do. The same idea of completion, of meeting a preconceived standard, of attaining an end, occurs in the prose works and in *Paradise Lost, Paradise Regained,* and *Samson Agonistes* when Milton is speaking of things, but not of persons or the Deity. In *Paradise Lost,* for example, "a perfect Phalanx," [117]

[117] Book I, l. 550.

"perfet ranks," [118] "perfet formes," [119] "perfet beauty," [120] "perfet sight," [121] "perfect image," [122] "perfet Gold," [123] "perfet miserie," [124] and a fabric of "absolute perfection" [125] are all easy to interpret in their expression of a standard reached or totality. In *Paradise Regained,* similarly, "a perfect Dove," [126] "the perfect shape," [127] and "the perfet season" [128] imply attainment of a preconceived standard. In *Samson Agonistes* Samson prefers the liberty of gaol to the "perfet thraldom" [129] of life with Dalila. In *The Reason of Church Government Urged against Prelaty* the "perfect freedom" of the service of God expressed in the liturgy is contrasted with the "perfect slavery" [130] that prevails in the service of prelaty; and with Arcadian repetition Milton asks, "Is not a farre more perfect worke more agreeable to his perfection in the most perfect state of the Church militant, the new alliance of God to man?" [131] In that sentence, however, the word *perfection* is used in a far different sense from *completion.* In *Eikonoklastes* every true church is declared to be "complete and perfet within it self." [132] In *Of Reformation in England* the statement that in England the Reformation should have "sooner attain'd Perfection" [133] plainly means completion. In *The Christian Doctrine* the words *perfect* and *perfection* occur more frequently than in any other single work, and there, too, they are sometimes used to express their original meaning, that of completeness. Such references as those to "works . . . as perfect as the nature of the subject will admit," [134] the "perfect shape" of Truth,[135] and the "two things necessary to constitute a perfect action, motion and the effect of motion," [136] are further evidence of the meaning of completeness. In his use of the term to imply completion, however, Milton does not hesitate to speak of degrees of perfection—a conception illogical to the ancients. Though he says, in the *Doctrine and Discipline of Divorce,* that "what is more or less perfect we

[118] Book VI, l. 71.  [119] Book VII, l. 455.  [120] Book IV, l. 634.
[121] Book IV, l. 577.  [122] Book II, l. 764.  [123] Book V, l. 442.
[124] Book VI, l. 462.  [125] Book X, l. 483.  [126] Book I, l. 83.
[127] Book III, l. 11.  [128] Book IV, l. 468.  [129] Line 946.
[130] Columbia Edition, III, 272.  [131] *Ibid.,* III, 191.
[132] *Ibid.,* V, 208.  [133] *Ibid.,* III, 6.  [134] *Ibid.,* XIV, 3.
[135] *Ibid.,* IV, 337.  [136] *Ibid.,* XV, 29.

dispute not," [137] he speaks, in *The Christian Doctrine,* of "more perfect knowledge of the will of God," [138] a "more perfect rule of conduct," [139] as well as of the "perfecter sex," [140] the "perfecter obedience" [141] required by the gospel than that required by the law, "most perfect satisfaction," [142] the "perfetest commandment," [143] man's duty to "endeavor what is perfectest," [144] and of "going on by degrees to perfection" in government.[145]

Such expressions, like those in the Bible in which *perfect* and *perfection* occur, ultimately lead to the problem of the meaning of perfection in relation to the nature of man and of God as well; and it is here that Milton's solution becomes apparent. The references to the perfection of God are few in number; those to the perfection of man are numerous. Beginning in the Anti-prelatical tracts, continuing through two of the divorce tracts, the *Doctrine and Discipline of Divorce* and *Tetrachordon,* and through *Of Education* and *Areopagitica,* the discussion of perfection is naturally fullest and most conclusive in *The Christian Doctrine, Paradise Lost,* and *Paradise Regained.*

Apparently the problem arises with the question of man's claims to perfection, for in the tract *Of Prelatical Episcopacy,* concerning the origin of episcopacy, whether human or divine, Milton cites the Scriptures as the only "Divine authority . . . setting out to us a perfect man of God, accomplish't to all the good workes of his charge." [146] Though the tract does not proceed to define the meaning of the phrase "a perfect man of God," it raises the question for later treatment. What the basis of Milton's solution is to be, however, is clear from the start: "But if any shall strive to set up his *Ephod,* and *Teraphim* of Antiquity against the brightnesse and perfection of the Gospell, let him feare lest he and his *Baal* be turn'd into

---

[137] *Ibid.,* III, 452.     [138] *Ibid.,* XVI, 149.     [139] *Ibid.,* XV, 175.
[140] *An Apology for Smectymnuus,* III, 306.
[141] *Doctrine and Discipline of Divorce,* Columbia Edition, III, 451.
[142] *The Christian Doctrine,* Columbia Edition, VI, 337.
[143] *Tetrachordon,* Columbia Edition, IV, 172.
[144] *Doctrine and Discipline of Divorce,* Columbia Edition, III, 470.
[145] *The Ready and Easy Way to Establish a Free Commonwealth,* Columbia Edition, VI, 132.     [146] Columbia Edition, III, 81.

*Bosheth.*" [147] In the *Animadversions upon the Remonstrant's Defence against Smectymnuus* the problem arises again, from a different angle. Here Christ is appealed to as the "perfect image of the Father," one who is a God, whose "nature is perfection," and who can "vouchsafe to us (though unworthy) as large a portion of thy spirit as thou pleasest." [148] That *perfection* here still savors of its ancient meaning of completion is evident, however, from the context: "O perfect and accomplish thy glorious acts! for men may leave their works unfinished, but thou art a God, thy nature is perfection." Similarly in *The Reason of Church Government* the question of the perfection of Christ and man is associated with the idea of completeness in Milton's attack on ceremony in church worship.[149] Such "polluted cloathing" of the "pure simplicity of doctrine" as church ceremony supplies "casts an ignominy upon the perfection of Christ's ministry"; and "in respect of ceremony which is but a rudiment of the Law, the weakest Christian hath thrown off the robes of his minority, and is a perfect man, as to legal rites." There is more than completeness implied here, however, for in Milton's later contrast between love and law as the source of excellence or perfection, he reaches the core of the New Testament meaning of the term. The prelaty, on the other hand, while pretending to "perfect [that is, complete] the church's unity . . . aspires and sharpens to ambition, not to perfection, or unity." [150] In *An Apology for Smectymnuus* Milton's expression of his determination to live an upright life, in order to write well, and his belief that he, as one of "the perfecter sex," must scorn incontinence, is the conclusion of a defense of himself that he says is "last of all, not in time, but as perfection is last" [151]—an expression that plainly indicates the two-fold meaning of attainment of a goal and moral excellence as well. In the remaining tracts the idea of moral excellence is seldom absent.

It is in the *Doctrine and Discipline of Divorce,* the *Tetrachordon,* and *The Christian Doctrine* that the problem of human and divine perfection comes out into the open, demanding some kind of solu-

[147] *Ibid.,* p. 104.  [148] *Ibid.,* pp. 147, 148.  [149] *Ibid.,* p. 247.
[150] *Ibid.,* p. 218.  [151] *Ibid.,* p. 305.

tion. At times Milton's statements seem vague or inconclusive or even contradictory, but in the end, in the light of *Paradise Lost* and *Paradise Regained,* the solution is clear. In a sense all of Milton's works relate to or illustrate his belief in human and divine excellence, but it is necessary to study his explicit statements concerning the problem of perfection in order to define his conclusions.

In the *Doctrine and Discipline of Divorce* and the *Tetrachordon* it is the question of man's claims to perfection that is again raised, with little or no reference to the perfection of God. In the *Doctrine and Discipline of Divorce,* after citing Homer, Plato and the Peripatetics, Chrysippus and other Stoics, and Cicero and Manilius in defense of the law of nature and in proof of the contention that the "justice of God stood upright ev'n among heathen disputers"; [152] after quoting Old and New Testament passages to prove that Moses, the prophets, and Christ approved of divorce, whether by law or the gospel; after citing Augustine, Philo, Maimonides, Calvin, Beza, Pareus, Selden, and others as authorities who controverted or supported his thesis of the necessity of man's dependence on his own right reason and free will in the matter of divorce; after turning his attention briefly to the too strict discipline of some of the sects concerning divorce—Milton expresses the following beliefs concerning human perfection: before the Fall, man and woman were perfect; [153] natural law, which, because it is God's law, is perfect, was established in the time of man's original perfection; [154] after the Fall, God gave men no new laws concerning marriage and divorce because, while "framing their laws and them to all possible perfection," [155] he expected man to "look back upon the first institution, that he may endeavour what is perfectest"; [156] though the Bible does not command perfection and man is nowhere required to achieve the perfection of Paradise, the law of the Old Testament was given to "help man forward to perfection," [157] and "the Gospell . . . exhorts to highest perfection but beares with weakest infirmity more than the Law." [158] In one instance, Milton's defense of natural

152 *Ibid.,* p. 442.　　153 *Ibid.,* pp. 441, 456, 457.　　154 *Ibid.,* p. 457.
155 *Ibid.,* p. 465.　　156 *Ibid.,* pp. 465, 470.　　157 *Ibid.,* p. 482.
158 *Ibid.,* p. 451.

law leads him to ask how man can imitate God, to *"be perfect as he is perfect,"* if man disregards the law,[159] suggesting that Christ's charge to his disciples was one of the first sources of Milton's concern with the whole problem of human perfection. Another very interesting and revealing comment on the problem occurs in connection with Milton's reference to Christ's parable of the Rich Young Ruler. According to Milton, Christ, in Matthew 19:21, in telling the young man to "sell that thou hast and give to the poor" if he wished to be perfect, did not wish "to contend with the arrogant young man who boasted his observance of the whole Law, whether he had indeed kept it or not, but skrues him up higher, to a task of that perfection, which no man is bound to imitate." [160] The reference is revealing for its evidence that thus early Milton was thinking of perfection as a matter of growth, a way of life, rather than as a completion or a goal attained, and also that thus early he was aware of the fact that man's pursuit of perfection must always be a matter of free choice. Later, in *The Christian Doctrine,* he cites the same parable with the same conclusions. This "self-sufficient young man," says Milton, was thus severely answered by Christ "for the purpose of exposing his folly and unfounded confidence, and of showing him how far he was from the perfection to which he pretended. For it was not the selling all he had, which has been done without charity, but the leaving his possessions and following Christ, which was to be the test of his perfection." [161] Above all, the parable reveals the core of all Milton's later doctrine concerning human perfection, namely, that charity, or love, is "the bond of perfection." "The Gospel," he says, "enjoyns no new morality, save only the infinit enlargement of charity"; and "it is no command of perfection further than it partakes of charity, which is *the bond of perfection."* [162] Thomas Aquinas had clearly stated the same idea, as had others before him.[163] Not wisdom or fortitude or patience or the sum of all the virtues would produce perfection, he said, but only love, which, in the words of Paul, is "the bond of perfection." [164]

[159] *Ibid.,* p. 446.     [160] *Ibid.,* p. 457.     [161] *Ibid.,* XVII, 19.
[162] *Ibid.; Doctrine and Discipline of Divorce,* III, 482.
[163] Cf. Garrigou-Lagrange, *op. cit.,* pp. 138–39.     [164] Colossians 3:14.

In the *Tetrachordon* Milton again emphasizes the idea that the "rule of perfection . . . is nearest to the rule of charity," [165] and he calls Christian love and charity "the summe of all commands and the perfection." [166] The man who "forgoes an unfit, ungodly & discordant wedloc, to live according to peace & love," rather than "live a contentious, and unchristian life," is more "in the way to perfection," so far as Milton is concerned.[167] In *Of Education* again he speaks of repairing "the ruines of our first Parents by regaining to know God aright, and out of the knowledge to love him, to be like him, as we may the neerest by possessing our souls of true vertue, which being united to the heavenly grace of faith makes up the highest perfection." [168] Love, virtue, faith together produce perfection, but the "greatest of these" is love.

Before writing *The Christian Doctrine* and *Paradise Lost,* therefore, Milton had already determined what to him were the meaning and the bases of human perfection. It was no end to be attained; rather it was a gradual progress toward an infinite excellence that could be conceived and imitated only by means of love. Being on the way was important. No end was to be achieved, simply because no end was conceivable. All that need concern mankind was that step by step it become better and better; and to the possibilities of becoming better there was no end. The fact that to evil there is likewise no end is expressed by Satan, whose evil increases step by step but is never completed:

> Which way I fly is hell; myself am hell;
> And in the lowest deep a lower deep
> Still threatening to devour me opens wide.[169]

The infinite possibilities of evil, however, served chiefly to stress the infinite possibilities of good—and the infinite possibilities of goodness, rather than evil, were to be Milton's central theme in all his later works. The idea is, as I have pointed out,[170] the out-

[165] Columbia Edition, IV, 172.　　[166] *Ibid.*, p. 186.
[167] *Ibid.*, p. 172.　　[168] *Ibid.*, p. 277.
[169] *Paradise Lost,* Book IV, ll. 75–77. Cf. Tsanoff, *loc. cit.*, p. 34.
[170] Cf. p. 96 above.

growth of the Greek ideal of Becoming, which led to the Christian concept of Infinity, not as chaos, but as a way, toward good or evil, according to the choice of the individual.

In *The Christian Doctrine* Milton reasserts his belief in the possibility of human perfection. Again he speaks of the "primitive perfection" [171] with which mankind was created, a perfection in which God does not preserve angels or men or "any other part of creation," except as they will to be preserved in it. He reaffirms the fact that Christian perfection is not to be forced [172] and that in the Bible "perfection is proposed to all men as the end of their endeavors," though "it is not required of all." [173] He interprets Paul's desire "to be with Christ" as a desire "to obtain immediate possession of heavenly perfection," [174] though such "perfection and consummation" [175] are to be achieved only after death. In his discussion of the sources of human perfection, he reasserts the efficacy of love and faith. The gifts and sacrifices offered in the Old Testament "could not make him that did the service perfect." [176] Good works are the natural evidence of faith, but "it is faith that justifies . . . faith is the essential form of good works," [177] as the parable of the Rich Young Ruler amply illustrates. But above all, love is again declared to be the "bond of perfection." Those who, "through a predominating regard to the law of love" [178] as taught in the New Testament, prove their love for God and neighbor by good works achieve a state "more perfect than those under the law," since they have "a more perfect knowledge of the will of God"; [179] and "So far from a less degree of perfection being exacted from Christians, it is expected of them that they should be more perfect than those who were under the law." [180] Milton is ever mindful of the fact that the Bible speaks of human perfection, as in the case of Noah, whom he later describes in *Paradise Lost* as "so perfet and so just." Of such references he says: "When a man is said to be perfect and just in the sight of God, this is to be understood according to the

---

[171] Columbia Edition, XV, 59.

[173] *Ibid.*, XVII, 21.

[176] *Ibid.*, p. 101.

[179] *Ibid.*, XVI, 149.

[174] *Ibid.*, XV, 241.

[177] *Ibid.*, XVII, 9.

[180] *Ibid.*, p. 151.

[172] *Ibid.*, p. 159.

[175] *Ibid.*, XVI, 97.

[178] *Ibid.*

measure of human righteousness, and as compared with the progress of others; or it may mean that they were endued with a sincere and upright heart, without dissimulation." [181] Here he plainly thinks of perfection as a matter of growth, not of completion. His uncertainty as to the "measure" or degree of human righteousness attainable is also clear, however; and when he adds the last clause, suggesting a simpler alternative meaning, his uncertainty is even clearer. The most complete statement of Milton's beliefs concerning human perfection in *The Christian Doctrine* occurs in Chapter XXI, "Of Being Ingrafted in Christ, and Its Effects." [182] The "spiritual increase" derived from such love or "ingrafting," he says, is the way to perfection, and here the quality of growth is again apparent. His following explicit definition of the nature of perfection, however, shows that he has accepted without qualification the doctrine of the Reformers:

> With regard to perfection, although not to be expected in the present life, it is our duty to strive after it with earnestness, as the ultimate object of our existence. . . . Hence the struggle between the flesh and the Spirit in the regenerate. . . . There is also a victory to be gained . . . over the world . . . over death . . . over Satan. Hence such as are strenuous in this conflict, and earnestly and unceasingly labor to attain perfection in Christ, though they be really imperfect, are yet, by imputation and through the divine mercy, frequently called in Scripture "perfect," and "blameless," and "without sin"; inasmuch as sin, though still dwelling in them, does not reign over them.[183]

At the time that this part of *The Christian Doctrine* was written, therefore, Milton was still unwilling to give his whole-hearted support to the doctrine of real, rather than imputed, perfection and of sinlessness in this life. If the Scriptures called Noah and others *perfect,* they did so only through a kindly wish to praise man's efforts toward godliness and to overlook his real imperfections.

Later, in *Paradise Lost* and *Paradise Regained,* no such reserva-

181 *Ibid.*          182 *Ibid.*, p. 3.          183 *Ibid.*, pp. 19–23.

tions are expressed; for in the perfect state of Adam and Eve,[184] in the perfection of Noah,[185] in Raphael's assertion that all things are "created . . . such to perfection," [186] in God's characterization of Christ as "this perfect Man," [187] and in Christ's promise that his "Merit those human beings shall perfet," [188] the possibility of a sinless, perfect humanity seems assured. In fact, when doubt is expressed of man's perfection, it is put into the mouth of Satan: ". . . what of perfection can in man be found or human nature can receive." [189] Spoken to Christ, the words are full of irony. The limitations of the perfection of the ancients, in their ignorance of themselves and of God, are asserted by Christ to Satan:

> The Stoic last in Philosophic pride,
> By him call'd vertue; and his vertuous man,
> Wise, perfect in himself, and all possessing
> Equal to God.[190]

Such proud, self-righteous faith in the attainment or completion of perfection is not for the Christian. His way is one of love and faith and service, revealed to him by "Light from above, from the fountain of light." [191] Finally, then, Milton's faith in human perfection is practically identical with that of Arminius, the Cambridge Platonists, and the sectaries to whom sinlessness and real perfection were possible in this life for all who were guided by the Inner Light. As is to be expected, woman, to Milton, was never to attain the degree of perfection possible to man. God, in *Paradise Lost,* tells Adam that his "perfection far excell'd hers in all real dignity"; [192] and Eve finds Adam's goodness "ingaging me to emulate, but short of thy perfection." [193] Eve is "adorned with all perfections," [194] but, in the plural, they are aesthetic rather than moral.

The concept of infinite goodness naturally led philosophers and

---

[184] *Paradise Lost,* Book V, l. 524; Book VIII, l. 642.
[185] *Ibid.,* Book XI, l. 876.
[186] *Ibid.,* Book V, l. 472.
[187] *Paradise Regained,* Book I, l. 166.
[188] *Paradise Lost,* Book XI, ll. 36–37.
[189] *Paradise Regained,* Book III, l. 230.
[190] *Ibid.,* Book IV, ll. 300–4.
[191] *Ibid.,* Book IV, l. 289.
[192] *Paradise Lost,* Book X, l. 150.
[193] *Ibid.,* Book IX, l. 964.
[194] *Ibid.,* l. 1031.

theologians alike to contemplation of the nature of God and the angels. In the assertion that "infinite excellence . . . constitutes the true perfection of God," [195] Milton stresses the fundamental Christian concept of infinity. God's eternity, infinity, and unity are essential to the concept of divine perfection.[196] God, limited in any way, becomes a thing, imperfect in its completion and divisibility. God, to Milton, is, above all, Spirit, "that most perfect essence by which God subsists by himself, in himself, and through himself." [197] As such, he is above and beyond human comprehension or intellectual limitation. "It is impossible to comprehend accurately under any form of definition of the 'divine nature,' " [198] says Milton, simply because man is finite and God is infinite. He is "Love without end, and without measure Grace." [199] Nevertheless, to deny God growth in perfection, while ascribing such perfectibility to man, would be to limit God's perfection. To Milton, therefore, God is "the living God," [200] who, though he is declared to be immutable in *The Christian Doctrine,*[201] in *Paradise Lost* grows toward greater and greater excellence in the light of new experience. Finding that "farr the greater part have kept, I see, thir station" [202] in heaven, after the fall of the rebel angels, God determines to create "another world, out of one man a Race of men innumerable," [203] whose will is free and who therefore provide him with more experience. Adam's request for a mate, after the Creation, reveals to God man's "single imperfection," [204] that of loneliness. To God's inquiry as to why Adam, created in God's image, is not happy, Adam replies, "Thou in thy self art perfet, and in thee is no deficience found." [205] Here the idea seems to be that of completeness; but Adam has just spoken of "the highth and depth of thy Eternal wayes," of which "all human thoughts come short," [206] so that the idea of infinite excellence

[195] *The Christian Doctrine,* Columbia Edition, XIV, 61.
[196] Cf. Foss, *op. cit.,* p. 19 n. 13.
[197] *The Christian Doctrine,* Columbia Edition, XIV, 43.
[198] *Ibid.,* XIV, 39.      [199] *Paradise Lost,* Book III, l. 142.
[200] *The Christian Doctrine,* Columbia Edition, XIV, 31–43.
[201] *Ibid.,* p. 47.      [202] *Paradise Lost,* Book VII, ll. 145–46.
[203] *Ibid.,* ll. 155–56.      [204] *Ibid.,* Book VIII, l. 423.
[205] *Ibid.,* ll. 415–16.      [206] *Ibid.,* ll. 413–14.

remains. In his final response to Adam's request, God discovers that "a nice and suttle happiness I see thou to thyself proposest," [207] and Adam's request is granted. Satan, brooding over his own fall and the imminent fall of man, reveals again God's growth as Creator:

> O Earth, how like to Heav'n, if not preferr'd
> More justly, Seat worthier of Gods, as built
> With second thoughts, reforming what was old!
> For what God after better worse would build? [208]

In Michael's account of man's history after the Fall, God is said to become "at last wearied with their iniquities" and to "withdraw his presence from among them" and to resolve "from thenceforth to leave them to their own polluted wayes," [209] except for Abraham and his "race elect." In time the race elect likewise grows "factious," [210] loses its power, and "God with man unites" [211] in the person of Christ, the "perfect man," who is to prove, through love and suffering, the perfectibility of humankind as well as the infinite love and justice of God, the Father. Adam's ecstatic vision of such "goodness infinite, goodness immense" [212] is ample assurance that paradise is not lost, that, by the grace of a living God, mankind is on the way to a new paradise, and that "meditation on the happie end," [213] rather than actual completion or attainment, is the source of man's perpetual blessing.

Thus Milton's ideas concerning perfection, like his solutions of other issues of his day, are found to be his own reasoned convictions, deduced mainly from his study of the Scriptures but influenced by the views of his predecessors and contemporaries. In his acceptance of the doctrine of love as the "bond of perfection," he took his stand with Christ, Paul, Augustine, Thomas Aquinas, and all the Christian theologians, both Catholic and Protestant, to whom Christ's two commandments, to love God and neighbor, were the means of the fulfilling of the law. In his denial, in *The Christian Doctrine,* of the

[207] *Ibid.,* ll. 399–400.
[208] *Ibid.,* Book IX, ll. 99–102.
[209] *Ibid.,* Book XII, ll. 107–13.
[210] *Ibid.,* l. 352.
[211] *Ibid.,* l. 382.
[212] *Ibid.,* l. 469.
[213] *Ibid.,* l. 605.

possibility of sinlessness in this life he agreed with Luther, Calvin, Episcopius, and such Quakers as Robert Barclay and William Penn, and he disagreed with the early Church Fathers, Augustine, Thomas Aquinas, Melancthon, Arminius, the Cambridge Platonists, the General Baptists, and George Fox. Later, however, Milton, too, grants a degree of sinlessness or perfection in this life and thus returns to Catholic doctrine at the same time that he accepts that of the sectaries. In many instances, as we have seen, the views of medieval Catholics and the sects agreed. Concerning the matter of real or imputed perfection, Milton first agrees with the Reformers in their doctrine of imputed perfection; later to Milton, as to Arminius, the Cambridge Platonists, and the sects, man's perfection is real, the result of his own free choice of the good. Such perfection is a way of life, to Milton as to Duns Scotus and all who followed him; and it was thus attainable by degrees, as Augustine, Thomas Aquinas, Arminius, the Baptists, and the Quakers had taught, even up to the excellence of God. In his belief in the infinite excellence of God, Milton again followed Duns Scotus, rejecting the limitations imposed by Augustine and Thomas Aquinas. To Milton, as to the Reformers, faith, rather than works, was necessary to the true love of God and man; works were only the outward evidence of the inner light.

On the whole, Milton's attitude toward the question of perfection is one of reasoned conviction rather than dogma or doctrine. Concerning such theological issues as whether man may attain sinlessness in this life and whether perfection is real or imputed, he changed his mind because they seemed to be of little importance as compared with the all-important matter of man's finding as a goal in life the immense goodness of God and of choosing a way of life that will lead him to that excellence. All just and perfect men, he says, have helped to point the way, but none so well as Christ. Milton reveals at times his own dilemma concerning the use of the illogical term *perfection* in his attempts to define precisely what he wishes to convey by it. Like other Christian writers, however, he uses it to mean "excellence" and in so doing continues the Christian tradition, even while he differs with his predecessors as to issues involved. It is doubtful whether any one person has done more to interpret the meaning of Christianity to the world than has John Milton; and perhaps the chief part of that interpretation is his realization of the Christian meaning of *perfection*.

In the year 1651, when Milton's growing fame among European scholars first led them to visit him, one of his visitors was a German, Christopher Arnold, later Professor of History at Nuremberg. Arnold kept an autograph album, and in it Milton had written for him in Greek the ninth verse of the twelfth chapter of Second Corinthians: "I am made perfect in weakness." [214] Behind those words, for Milton, lay a world of meaning. In the light of centuries of thought on the problem of man's purpose and destiny in the world, they express simply, though profoundly, a faith in man's achievement of excellence through love and obedience and suffering.

In January, 1948, in an address before the Historical Society of Pennsylvania, Dr. Arthur M. Schlesinger pointed out that "man of the nineteenth century was conceived as rational and perfectible, borne along on the irresistible tide of progress," whereas "the twentieth century has rejected that conception and replaced it with a pessimistic view of man as essentially imperfect, very likely doomed to frustration and driven by forces beyond his control." [215] With such a concept of man, more pessimistic and belittling than that of the Middle Ages, what will the twentieth century contribute toward his spiritual growth? Can civilization survive in any age without its "dreamers of perfection"? Former President Romulo Gallegos of Venezuela, on the occasion of his receiving the honorary degree of Doctor of Laws at Columbia University, spoke of the future, when "a definitive, mutual understanding binding all our peoples" should unite the Americas and ultimately the world. Such unity is still distant, he added, but there should be "dreamers of perfection

---

[214] Masson, *op. cit.*, IV, 353.
[215] Reported in the New York *Herald-Tribune*, January 24, 1948.

in our midst to plan for it." [216] Today, as in Milton's day, the true dignity of man is at stake. Again the world must choose between a dynamic faith in the fundamental goodness and worth of humankind and a static negation of the possibility of such excellence. Again, as in Milton's day, future history will depend on the choice.

[216] Reported in the New York *Times,* July 10, 1948.

# INDEX

Adam and Eve, joint hero of *Paradise Lost*, 69n, 71, 80, 81, 82-83, 86, 87, 88; perfection of, before the Fall, 108, 110-11, 122, 125, 127

Addison, Joseph, his objection to learning in *Paradise Lost*, 70, 71, 88, 90; on the theme of *Paradise Lost*, 71

*Animadversions upon the Remonstrant's Defence against Smectymnuus*, Milton's use of the term *perfection* in, 121

Anne of Cleves, promised to Henry VIII, 32; marriage of, to Henry VIII, 33; rejected by Henry VIII, 33; Stigel's epigrams to, 35; praised in Stigel's Epithalamium, 35, 40; pomp of her departure for England, 39-40

*Apology for Smectymnuus, An*, Milton's use of the term *perfection* in, 120n, 121

Aquinas, Thomas, *De Regimine Principum*, 45, 49n, 50n, 51n, 52n, 60; his definition of *perfection*, 95, 96, 101-2, 123, 129

*Areopagitica*, on Christian liberty, 82; on the need of learning, 91-92; defense of sects in, 114; Milton's use of the term *perfection* in, 120

Aristotle, *Politics*, 47, 53; idea of perfection in *Metaphysics*, 94, 102

Arminius, *see* Hermans, Jacobus

Arnold, Matthew, on the theme of *Paradise Lost*, 75; his definition of culture, 113

*Astrophel*, Spenser's expression of admiration for Rosalinde in, 3

Atonement, meaning of, 111

Augsburg Confession, 103

Augustine, on the nature of sin, 91; on the nature of perfection, 100-1, 129; read by Thomas Ellwood, 116; cited on divorce, 122

Bacon, Francis, *Advancement of Learning*, 89

Bagehot, Walter, on the theme of *Paradise Lost*, 74-75

Banks, Theodore, "Spenser's Rosalinde: a Conjecture," 12

Baptist movement, the, origin of Quakerism in, 107-10; Arminian nature of, 108; Milton's tenets like those of, 108; early history of, 108-10, 113; Milton's idea of perfection unlike that of, 130

Barclay, Robert, 106, 107n, 112n, 113, 130

Barker, Arthur, *Milton and the Puritan Dilemma*, 15n; quoted, 81, 82

Bartholomew the Englishman, *Bestiary*, 49n

Baumer, Franklin Le V., *Early Tudor Theory of Kingship*, 31-32n

Bees, government of, 49-50, 57, 61

Bennett, Josephine Waters, *The Evolution of the Faerie Queene*, 4n

Bible, the, as the source of *Paradise Lost*, 80, 83-84, 88, 95; use of the term *perfection* in, 96-98, 120, 121, 122, 123, 125, 126; Milton's chief source, 99, 118, 125, 129

"Bigge Bulles of Basan," 23, 27

Blake, William, his interpretation of *Paradise Lost*, 74

Body Politic, the, 49, 57

Braithwaite, William C., *The Second Period of Quakerism*, 106n, 113n;

by, 103, 111; influence of, on Robert Barclay, 113; Milton's agreement with, 126, 130

Macaulay, Rose, *Milton,* 68n, 78
Macaulay, Thomas Babington, comment of, on *Paradise Lost,* 74
Making of the greater man, the, as the theme of *Paradise Lost,* 69-70, 78-79, 82-93, 120-31; universality of the theme of, 70, 71-72, 131-32; timeliness of the theme of, 70, 93, 131-32
Mantuan's ninth eclogue, relation of, to Spenser's September eclogue, 24n
Marian exiles, 21, 28n
*Marian Exiles, The* (Garrett), 15n
Marsilius of Padua, 31, 45, 46n, 50n, 53, 54, 65
Masson, David, *Life of Milton,* first volume published, 74; influence of sects on Milton discussed in, 98-99n, 117-18; comment of, on Thomas Ellwood, 115; Milton's autograph verse, recorded by, 131
McGiffert, A. C., *Protestant Thought before Kant,* 79n, 84n
McLane, Paul E., supports the suggestion of Richard Davies as Diggon Davie, 21-23
McMahon, A. Philip, "Sidney's Letter to the Camerarii," 24n, 26n, 27n, 28n
*Means to Remove Hirelings out of the Church,* Milton's defense of sects in, 114
Melancthon, Philip, 26n, 32, 33, 34, 40; meaning of perfection to, 103-4, 130
Miller, Perry, *The Puritans,* 15n
*Milton Handbook, A* (Hanford), 80n, 95n, 98n, 106n
Milton, John, critics of, 66-82; Puritanism of, 71, 73, 75, 79, 80, 81, 83, 95; humanism of, 78, 79, 80, 81, 93, 95; perfectibilitarianism of, 84-86, 87; relation of, to Spenser, 92-93; sectarianism of, 108-9; definition of

perfection by, like that of George Fox, 111; defense of sects by, 114; acquaintance of, with sectaries, 115-18; use of the term *perfection* by, in *Paradise Lost,* 111-12, 118-19, 126-29; in minor poems, 118; in *Samson Agonistes,* 118-19; in prose works, 118-26; in *Paradise Regained,* 118-19, 126-29; definition of perfection by, like that of Arminius, the Cambridge Platonists, the sectaries, 127; definition of perfection by, the result of his reasoned convictions, 129-30
Minor Poems of Milton, idea of perfection in, 118
*Mixed Essays, Irish Essays, and Others* (Arnold), 75n
Monarchy, Continental theory of, 31, 41, 51; Tudor development of, 31, 49; Stigel's theories of, 38-40; evils of, 43; medieval theories of, in *Mum and the Sothsegger,* 43, 65; meaning of the term, 44-45; conflict of, with Papacy and Empire, 44-45, 51; need for, 45, 48, 52; advantages of, 48, 49; argument for, from the Body Politic, 49; argument for, from natural phenomena, 49-50; argument for, from the example of Jhengiz Khan, 50; election in, 54; contractual relation in, 57; necessity of allegiance in, 57, 63-64; reason approves, 62; dependent on law, 65; advantages of limited, 65
Monastics, meaning of perfection to, 100; objections to the perfection of, 102, 103
More, Henry, depended for perfection on reason and experience, 105-6; spiritual adviser of Lady Conway, 106; friend of Descartes, 106
More, Paul Elmer, "The Theme of *Paradise Lost,*" 68n, 77
*Mum and the Sothsegger,* 17n, 19; a poem of estates, 42-43; the author's